Robert J Maxwell

The Quest for Excellence

What is good health care?

Essays in honour of
Robert J Maxwell

by
Richard Best, Karen Davis, David J Hunter, Ken Judge,
Rudolf Klein, Alan Maynard, Marshall Marinker,
Fiona Moss, Patrick Nairne, Richard Smith,
Nicholas Timmins, David Towell, Albert Weale

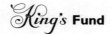

Published by
King's Fund Publishing
11–13 Cavendish Square
London W1M 0AN

© King's Fund 1998

First published 1998

ISBN 1 85717 146 2

A CIP catalogue record for this book is available from the British Library

Distributed by Grantham Book Services Limited
Isaac Newton Way
Alma Park Industrial Estate
GRANTHAM
Lincolnshire
NG31 9SD

Tel: 01476 541 080
Fax: 01476 541 061

Printed and bound in Great Britain by
Biddles Ltd, Guildford and King's Lynn

Frontispiece photograph: Laurie Sparham

Contents

List of contributors

Richard Best, OBE, Director, Joseph Rowntree Foundation

Karen Davis, President, The Commonwealth Fund

David J Hunter, Professor of Health Policy and Management,
The Nuffield Institute of Health

Ken Judge, Professor of Social Policy, PSSRU,
University of Kent at Canterbury

Rudolf Klein, Professor of Social Policy, University of Bath, and
Professorial Fellow, King's Fund Policy Institute

Alan Maynard, Professor of Health Economics, York Health
Economics Consortium, University of York

Marshall Marinker, OBE, Visiting Professor, United Medical and
Dental Schools of Guy's and St Thomas', University of London

Fiona Moss, Editor, *Quality in Health Care*, and Consultant Physician,
Central Middlesex Hospital NHS Trust

The Rt. Hon. Sir Patrick Nairne, Former Chairman, Nuffield Council
on Bioethics

Richard Smith, Editor, *British Medical Journal*

Nicholas Timmins, Public Policy Editor, *Financial Times*

David Towell, Fellow in Health Policy and Development, King's Fund
Management College

Albert Weale, Professor of Government, University of Essex

Foreword

The essays in the book celebrate the work and achievements of Robert Maxwell on the occasion of his retirement as Secretary and Chief Executive of the King's Fund, a position he has held since 1980.

The title chosen for this book, *The Quest for Excellence: What is good health care?*, reflects the values of both the King's Fund and of Robert Maxwell. The breadth of the subjects chosen by the thirteen distinguished contributors is also an attempt to capture something of the breadth of a colleague who has made significant contributions to health care reform, ethics, quality and standards, analysis, education and development; whose writing career began as a student at New College, Oxford, winning the Newdigate University Prize for poetry, and whose last major essay as Chief Executive of the King's Fund was an influential monograph on the 1996 BSE/CJD crisis!

Robert Maxwell's appointment to the King's Fund as Secretary and Chief Executive to succeed the eminent NHS administrator, Geoffrey Phalp, was a natural progression for one who had played an important role in the development of health policy during the late 1960s and 1970s. As a partner in the consultancy firm of McKinsey & Co., Robert Maxwell was a senior adviser to the Government during the health and social services changes which led to the large-scale reorganisation of the Department of Health & Social Security in 1974. His first book, *Health Care: The growing dilemma*, an international comparative study of health services, was published to great acclaim in 1974. From this grew Robert's direct involvement in the world of health care, first as administrator to the Special Trustees of St Thomas' Hospital – responsible for formidable hospital trust funds – and thence to the King's Fund.

Robert's second major book, *Health and Wealth*, published by Lexington Books in 1981, was a ground-breaking study of health expenditures across the developed world. Written at the end of the 1970s, the decade of world financial crises and high inflation, its analysis might seem equally pertinent today, as health systems throughout the developed world search for ways of reconciling rising costs and expectations with the need to contain public spending. Robert Maxwell's views on the National Health Service from this international perspective are captured in an interview with *The Lancet* in 1975:

> I suspect that we would find it impossible to recreate the fundamental decency and common sense of the NHS at its best: its dedication to equity of care; its emphasis on medicine as a caring profession not a business; and its impressive record (by international standards) of value for money. If the NHS breaks down, any alternative is likely to be less equitable, more mercenary, and a great deal more expensive.

Within a few years of arriving at Palace Court, Robert Maxwell had transformed the quiet haven of the King's Fund at Bayswater into a dynamic creative force, appointing a new management development team led by the late Tom Evans at the King's Fund College; stimulating new programmes in audit and community care in the King's Fund Centre; and, in 1986, establishing the King's Fund Institute, as a centre for independent policy analysis. It was through this range of new, relevant and challenging work for the health service that the King's Fund in the 1980s built its formidable reputation as a leading centre for health policy analysis, development and education, as well as for grants to the many voluntary organisations which work in the often unglamorous and neglected areas of health care.

As Robert Maxwell reported to the Fund's General Council in 1986:

> The Fund must not simply do things that are uncontroversial and safe. The only justification for its privilege and relative wealth, is if its independence is used in areas that are difficult and controversial ... leverage and selectivity are crucial. We therefore need constantly to question where our limited intervention can do most good, while recognising that activities have to be sustained over a sufficient period to have worthwhile impact.

As well as leading the King's Fund, Robert Maxwell continued to play a major role in developing ideas to shape health service delivery. His famous paper on 'Quality Assessment in Health', published in the *British Medical Journal* in May 1984, defined the dimensions of health care quality, which quickly became known as the 'Maxwell Six': access, relevance, effectiveness, equity, acceptability and efficiency. Collectively, these are still widely seen as the basic parameters for describing excellence in health care.

For many years Robert Maxwell has also been a Justice of the Peace for Inner London, chairing the Family and Youth Courts, and, among other appointments, he is a non-executive director of Lewisham Hospital: once the 'poor relation' to the mighty Guy's Hospital. His leadership of the Fund has often been directed to championing disenfranchised and silent groups, whether in supporting better health care for homeless people (a recurring concern of the King's Fund); or highlighting the health care needs of black and minority ethnic groups; or investigating the needs of carers and relatives. And at the same time Robert has not been frightened of generating controversy when he felt that there was an issue of principle or an example of good practice to be followed. Applying his own motto that 'it is easier to seek forgiveness than permission', he has led the King's Fund boldly through the difficult seas of London health care, and has been a calm and supportive leader to many a hesitant colleague. There are numerous people, in support of or opposition to the Fund's work through the years, who will remember how Robert's unfailing courtesy has so often disarmed the most energetic protagonist!

The subjects chosen in this collection of essays to Robert Maxwell thus attempt to reflect different aspects of a person who led the King's Fund to its present position as one of the pre-eminent and influential independent health care institutions in the UK; one whose influence now reaches far outside its original roots in the health services and health care of the people of London.

Richard Best begins the collection by looking at the role of foundations in modern Britain and comparing and contrasting the fortunes of the King's Fund and the Rowntree Foundation, on whose council Robert has sat for some years.

Four views of health care reform follow. Health care in the USA is examined by Karen Davis, who takes stock of the failure of the Clinton health reforms and looks at issues of health equity. David Hunter looks at the past 25 years and asks how much other European health care systems can learn from the health care reforms in the UK and how much we in the UK can learn from Europe. Alan Maynard views the same 25 years for the contribution of health economics, from its early work on budget allocations and outcome measurements to present issues in the economic evaluation of health care. Then Nicholas Timmins remembers an afternoon at the Department of Health in July 1993 when the architect of NHS management, Sir Roy Griffiths, began to reflect on the Conservative Government's 1991 health service reforms.

Changing relationships in the organisation and delivery of health care is the subject of the next four essays. Rudolf Klein critically examines the debate about a supposed 'democratic deficit' in the NHS and asks what this tells us about centre–periphery relationships. Marshall Marinker reviews five decades of concepts of care in general practice and suggests that today's descriptions of institutions and professions are now strained by new ideas and new behaviours in health care. He concludes with a personal view of the future of general practice. Richard Smith reflects on the wide range of possible influences, internal and external, that shape the way in which doctors go about their business. David Towell reviews the findings of the recent King's Fund London Commission and draws on social science theories for some practical lessons for transforming London's health system in the next five years.

The final four essays discuss aspects of the values in modern health care. Ken Judge takes a close look at uses of international comparisons of health inequalities, to show that drawing simple relationships does not stand up to scrutiny. Fiona Moss revisits Maxwell's dimensions of health care quality and looks at how quality of care in the NHS has improved over the past decade. Sir Patrick Nairne, first Chairman of the Nuffield Committee on Bioethics, reviews the work of the Committee over its first five years and examines progress in bioethical issues, particularly genetic screening and transplantation. Finally, Albert Weale examines the principles of a comprehensive, publicly funded health service and wonders whether the modern problems of costs and rationing of health care jeopardise the founding principles of the NHS.

King's Fund
London
November 1997

The influence of foundations

Why should policy-makers take any notice of foundations?

Richard Best OBE
Director, Joseph Rowntree Foundation

Foundations great and small

Most grant-making foundations are detached from the world's harsh realities: while everyone else seeks to make ends meet, wrestles for resources, fights cuts in funding and is never sure where the money will come from, the endowed foundations have a deep-seated security, in perpetuity. Theirs is an agenda which primarily addresses the distribution – not the raising – of funds. Outside of politics and insulated from the constraints that impinge daily upon virtually all private, voluntary and statutory bodies, what can the foundations know about the modern world? Why should anyone listen to them?

Distinctions

To begin, some distinctions must be made between the many varieties of foundations. First, I am discussing here only those with resources from their founders – which may have been multiplied by good investment, or diminished by ineptitude, over the years. And even these foundations come in many varieties.

Dead or alive

The next division is between those whose founders (or close kin) are still alive and prominent in their affairs and those with founders who are long deceased and who – while no doubt continuing to command gratitude and deference from those spending the money – do not impinge upon the foundation's day-to-day management.

Living founders may bring inspiration and enthusiasm. They may also be eccentric: they are unlikely to have been brought up and trained in the world of charity – they have been busy making money. They may be influenced by fashions and fads, or by people who fête them and woo them for funds. Spending can become whimsical or, worse, may be used to buy prestige, influence and honours. Some of those who create endowed charities will stand clear and allow expert trustees – and officers, if these can be afforded – to handle the work. But such founders seem a rare breed. More often their foundation becomes their hobby. The influence of these foundations is likely to be an extension – for good or ill – of the individual concerned.

There is much to be said for a dead founder. Power is then spread and shared between trustees (and officers). Some checks and balances are likely to evolve. Individual weakness and personal prejudice will be moderated by the involvement of a team. But the downside is that the potential influence of some dynamic characters – backed by money which must be spent – is lost to the public arena.

Words and deeds

The third distinction between foundations lies in the small print of their Trust Deeds. They can only do what their founders decided for them (and, mostly, the Charity Commission will resist latter-day proposals for significant changes). But frequently Trust Deeds are couched in the broadest terms – 'to do all things charitable' – and there is latitude to interpret and amend constitutional niceties.

Critical mass

A fourth, and very obvious, difference is the size of their endowment. The Wellcome Trust has billions; many endowed foundations hold only thousands. I am doubtful whether there is a close correlation between influence and income. But there is a sharp distinction between those with sufficient assets to afford high-level executive staff, and those for whom such management expenditure cannot be justified: the latter must rely – often with admirable results – on the voluntary input of their trustees. But when the critical mass is reached at which at least one senior officer can be appointed on a salary comparable to a senior civil servant or the chief executive of a national quango (or top-line voluntary body or local authority), then the potential of the organisation should move into a different gear. (Perhaps this means a minimum endowment of £50m at 1997 prices.)

Donating or doing

My final distinction concerns the extent to which the foundation decides to carry out executive functions, over and above the proper administration of its affairs. A foundation can act as a grant-maker and rely on those outside itself to take forward its objectives; or it can use its income – in full or part – to pursue its aims through the direct employment of staff. Most foundations prefer the first course, whether because they believe others will do the job better than they could or because they are uncomfortable with the relative inflexibility and potential hassle of taking the employment route.

The two foundations which I have chosen to illustrate my theme – the King's Fund and the Joseph Rowntree Foundation (JRF) – share similar characteristics:

- in both cases, the founding fathers – who were contemporaries at the turn of the century, a king and a businessman – are long gone. But through their line of succession, the founder still retains some influence. The King's Fund will receive a steer from its Royal President, now The Prince of Wales. For my foundation, Joseph Rowntree's enlightened writing continues to inspire, but physical presence is provided through his stipulation that half the trustees be appointed by the Society of Friends (Quakers). Only in critical moments do these historic connections have a clear impact upon the affairs of the organisation: but there is always the chance of decisive influence if a crisis strikes;

- both these bodies pursue objectives in fields of social welfare. The Trust Deed of the King's Fund directs its attention to issues of health, and confines its beneficiaries to the citizens of London. The JRF has scope to cover rather wider areas of social concern and can benefit citizens of the UK and the Commonwealth: in practice, its trustees have confined themselves to areas of known interest to the founder, including aspects of housing, poverty and care, and funds are confined to the UK. Not 'spreading the butter too thinly' is the underlining motive for these restrictions, linked to a belief that policy influence will be greatest in the areas where networks, experience and expertise are strongest;

- both the foundations are wealthy: the King's Fund with a capital base of around £140m in 1996, and the JRF with about £200m (and a further £50m of endowment tied up in its Housing Trust). With these resources, both can afford to recruit senior officers at salaries which will not deter those able to command senior positions elsewhere;

- both these organisations have resolved to spend significant proportions of their investment income on internal staffing, thereby diminishing the sums available for grants to external

4

bodies. Both supplement their income from external sources: in the case of the King's Fund, from government grants and from charging for activities, and in the case of the JRF, through its Housing Trust, in rental income and government grants.

Changing the world

Most foundations content themselves with using their resources to improve the lives of individuals. The money travels through local charities, voluntary bodies and community groups, to reach people in need – of care and attention, education, decent housing or a range of other services.

Sometimes a foundation's support for a local voluntary project, backed on its own merits, will have a wider impact. An example will be set; those concerned with a local charity will spread the word; other practitioners and, indeed, policy-makers may be affected. But wider change will be a bonus, on top of the support that reaches individuals in difficulty.

Most of the larger foundations recognise that they have a broader role in seeking to strengthen the charitable and voluntary sector as a whole. Unless the sector thrives, there will not be an outlet for good grant-making. And nurturing and supporting the sector are seen as important in themselves, in achieving greater pluralism and diversity than could be achieved if the State had to take direct responsibility for supplying the same needs.

Turning the telescope

A handful of foundations see the position from the other end of the telescope. While delighted that most charitable endeavour has direct consequences for people who would otherwise continue to suffer, they see their role as finding out why such suffering continues and suggesting the changes of policy and practice which may prevent it recurring.

The King's Fund and the JRF – and a few of our sister foundations – want to exert an influence for good among practitioners and policy-makers. This is a broader objective, and success is hard to achieve and even harder to assess.

The King's Fund has moved from the straightforward supply of funds to the voluntary hospitals of London, to the more subtle task of researching health needs and services, and seeking to establish sound policy and good practice. In 1947, the Duke of Gloucester asked, in the annual report, 'What is the King's Fund going to do with its money, now that the need to sustain the voluntary hospitals has passed into history?' He answered: 'The Fund has from its early days never accepted the view that its opportunities were limited to the mere distribution of grants. Taking into its counsels leaders in the hospital world of London, the Fund has been a centre of many new conceptions of the duties and responsibilities of the hospitals towards the community.'[1]

The Joseph Rowntree Foundation has been guided since 1904 by the vision of its founder to see beyond the curing of today's ills, to discovering their root causes so they can be tackled at their source. In his memorandum for the trustees who came after him, Joseph Rowntree wanted them 'to seek out the underlying causes of weakness or evil', to contribute to 'the right measures of human advancement' which over a period of time could 'change the face of England'.[2]

In these terms, the paths of the two charities have increasingly converged.

Foundations for change

On what authority can charitable bodies command the attention of those with power and responsibility in society?

Their case for change must be built upon the firm foundation of superior knowledge, hard evidence and the outcomes of independent investigation. The basis must be not whom you know, but what you know. Foundations can only expect others to change if the case they make has the credibility of rigorous underlying research and analysis. Most of the spending by the JRF goes to universities and other academic institutions to pursue the quest for truth about society's ills and about *what works* in tackling these. As well as evaluating developmental projects, a modest part of the total goes directly to the development work – since pioneering initiatives cannot be evaluated if they are not funded in the first place.

Similarly, the King's Fund supports R&D, commissioning independent evaluation alongside support for innovative local projects. The aim is to achieve models which can be replicated elsewhere. Good work at the local level – however important to those whom it helps – is only the means to the broader end, the achieving of change for the better.

Hands on

Diana Leat, in her publications on grant-making trusts, makes the distinction between those foundations that make gifts (and may only expect a polite 'thank you' in return) and those who enter into partnerships.[3] (In between come the foundations who see their donation as a social investment and hope that an evaluation will show that the work has produced good value for money.) The King's Fund and the JRF come into the 'hands-on' category of those who do not give presents but instead want to be part of the process, finding and funding partners on the outside.

When the JRF agrees to fund a project, it sees this as a beginning: we want to participate in the shaping of the work, in planning its outcomes at the beginning, in creating an advisory group to support the project's progress, and in following through at its conclusion, with further activity that may lead eventually to changes of policy and practice. For about 10 per cent of our projects we can link up with our housing association, the Joseph Rowntree Housing Trust (which owns some 2000 homes and attempts to pioneer new approaches to housing and care provision): we can then engage directly in innovative work, to find out what succeeds and what fails.

The King's Fund similarly maintains an overview of the research it supports, seeking always to detect the potential for changes in practice or policy, based on good evidence. Some of its research and evaluation will be undertaken in house through its own Policy Institute. And it is deeply involved in the processes of promoting improvements in the health services through its Development Centre (which draws in external funding from the NHS Executive).

These foundations are engaging directly in the quest, in partnership with others.

Horses to water

Charitable foundations cannot make the policy-makers and practitioners heed the messages that flow from the R&D which they fund. But they can make the process of obtaining and assimilating those messages as easy as possible. (There is always a danger for the generalist foundation of straying across the border line of charity law into the arena of 'campaigning', if too much pressure is exerted. The horse can be led to water and encouraged to drink but it should not be driven headlong into the lake!)

The most suitable form of dissemination will depend upon the audiences and their circumstances. But this part of the process of influencing decision-makers is likely to have some common components:

- summarising the findings from research projects (e.g. on four sides of A4, irrespective of how many thousands of words are contained in the main report), will invariably be helpful;
- use of plain English and clarity in the text are essential;
- ensuring that the summary reaches a wide audience of appropriate readers and, as necessary, attracts attention in the news media;
- investing in good design for the report;
- gaining coverage in technical and professional journals, to reach those who need to know.

Deeds not words

This is the point at which most independent sponsors of research, analysis and evaluation feel that their duty ends. The word has been disseminated competently: perhaps *The Independent* or *The*

Guardian has done a special feature; perhaps the report has had a mention on BBC Radio 4's *Today* programme; 500 copies of a good report have gone to an influential target audience; etc.

But has anything changed? Has the foundation's work actually influenced anyone to behave differently? Have deeds followed the words?

Foundation chief executives have two alibis, at this point: they can claim that they have raised the issue, provoked the debate, and their role is over; or they can rely on the argument that change takes time and – like water dripping on stone – the results will only be noticed years later. But in their hearts, those chief executives – and their trustees – may feel uneasy: has anyone noticed? Were the investment, the hard work of researchers and the added value of the foundation's input, all a waste of time?

In different ways, the JRF and the King's Fund have sought to persist. They have not been content to let matters lie.

The King's Fund has sought to engage directly with the key practitioners, providing consultancy and training through its Management College (with its Change and Leadership Centre, for example, and its creation of networks for the chief executives and senior doctors/nurses from major hospitals). Its Organisational Audit section translates the messages into measurements of good practice to achieve more effective ways of working (including through accreditation of health services). And the Development Centre works directly with health professionals to improve their effectiveness through encouraging the development of evidence-based practice and providing opportunities for discussion and debate. At the policy level, the Fund is trying to get practitioners to do things differently and, sometimes, to change their approach and attitude.

The JRF has also been increasingly concerned at the need to follow through once the initial publicity for a report has died down. We ask the question 'What next?' and wherever there seems more to be done, we devise an action plan:

- sometimes this will involve a relatively high-profile launch, perhaps with a government minister invited to respond;
- sometimes there will be a conference or series of seminars;
- sometimes direct links with a television company for one or more programmes may be worth pursuing; or a video to popularise the usual findings can be commissioned;
- sometimes a private presentation to ministers or senior civil servants will seem appropriate;
- sometimes there will be public 'road shows' for service users, practitioners and civic leaders.

But the JRF has also recognised the need to provide resources to organisations which themselves have the capacity for persistence, since it has not gone so far down the King's Fund route of direct employment of expert staff. Allowances have been formed with federations, professional institutions, associations and voluntary agencies.

Did it work?

The foundation has put time, money and energy into attempting to make its R&D achieve improvements in policies and practices, working in partnership not just with researchers and pioneering practitioners but with the news media and with skilled and committed individuals: but when can it say that it has, indeed, exerted some influence?

Seldom is the voice of the King's Fund or the JRF alone in the wilderness. Success is only likely if others are soon claiming the ideas as their own, politicians are adapting changes with their own personal touches, campaigners are advocating the measures under their own brand names. Unlike the others, the foundation does not need the credit to survive: no one pays it for the column-inches of newsprint it achieves; it is not dependent on votes for its continued existence; it does not need to impress sponsors and funders. It can afford to swallow its pride and allow others to collect the prizes.

But sometimes it may have been almost alone in championing some change of attitude, policy or practice: it may have espoused a cause which has had little or no political, public or popular support. Where, ultimately, its line has prevailed, perhaps the underlying influence it exerts in other spheres can be discerned.

In the mid-1980s, the Joseph Rowntree Foundation backed an inquiry, chaired by The Duke of Edinburgh (with the Foundation's chairman as his deputy); subsequently, the trustees stood behind the Inquiry's conclusions and recommendations, investing substantial further sums in supplementary research to underpin the earlier findings. Key conclusions included the firm proposal for a phasing-out of mortgage interest tax relief, with a shift in emphasis from the then-fashionable extension of home ownership and advocacy for not only investment in social housing (which others also championed) but for a new private rented sector (in which no political party took much interest). Within ten years, a Conservative government had largely removed the subsidy of tax relief for home owners and a little later a new Labour government proclaimed the virtues of a strong private rented sector. Of course, along the way, important allies were recruited, powerful advocates joined the fray and far-sighted politicians and opinion-formers took up the cause. But perhaps, for once, some credit can go to the foundation concerned (which, more than a decade later, continues to pursue some issues both in sponsoring new research on issues surrounding support for lower-income home owners and through practical demonstration of how new forms of private renting can work).[4, 5]

Similarly, the King's Fund can justifiably claim credit for seeing through significant health reforms, from the collection and analysis of evidence to the implementation of changed practice in the field. An example can be found in its programme on mental health and learning disabilities from 1970 onwards, which has contributed to changing these services from an institutional and paternalistic model to one that is community-based and much more geared to the choices inherent in an ordinary life.

No one should join a 'change-making' foundation in the hope of gaining personal glory, however diligently they may pursue the truth and however fervently they endeavour to see their quest translated

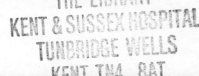

into better policies or practice. Only occasionally can the genuine influence of the foundation be perceived clearly. More often there will be the quiet satisfaction of noting the cause and effect without expecting others to recognise the genesis of the reform.

In conclusion

One of the guiding hands behind improvements to the lives of UK citizens has been Robert Maxwell in his role as Chief Executive of the King's Fund. Perhaps his natural tendency to be unassuming in seeking recognition for the influence he has exerted has been the ideal characteristic for the holder of his post. There is little doubt that the Fund has been a powerful – if often unacknowledged – force in the development of better policies and practices in the health service. And no chief executive – or founder – of a major charity can hope for more than this.

References
1. King's Fund. *100 years supporting people's health: centenary report*. London: King's Fund, 1997.
2. Barron D *et al*. *The JR trusts*. York: Joseph Rowntree Foundation, 1995.
3. Leat D. *Trusts in transition; Guide for Grant-givers*. York: Joseph Rowntree Foundation, 1990.
4. Inquiry into British Housing: National Federation of Housing Associations (1985); Second Report from the Inquiry into British Housing. York: Joseph Rowntree Foundation, 1991.
5. Best R *et al*. *The case for private renting*. York: Joseph Rowntree Foundation, 1994.

Equity
and
health
policy

Karen Davis
President, The Commonwealth Fund

Health systems in industrialised nations are increasingly the focus of governmental scrutiny. The desire to change current systems to achieve greater efficiency and reduce the share of economic and budgetary resources devoted to health care is driving this re-examination. In some countries, the health policy debate goes to the heart of the role of government in the financing and/or delivery of health care, and the extent of social solidarity versus individual responsibility for health care. The preoccupation with public spending inevitably focuses greater attention on improving the performance of health systems in terms of efficiency, at the possible sacrifice of equity.

Remarkably little cross-national health system analysis informs this health policy debate within individual countries. The pioneering work of Maxwell[1] demonstrated the value of comparative health policy analysis as a mechanism for facilitating informed decision-making by government policy officials in shaping national health systems to achieve the twin goals of equity and efficiency. In recent years, the Organization of Economic Cooperation and Development (OECD) has generated valuable data on cross-national health spending and utilisation of health care services, which help assess health system performance in terms of macro-efficiency.[2] An in-depth empirical examination of equity in the financing and receipt of health care services in ten countries, sponsored by the Commission of the European Communities Health Services Research Committee, also provides important insight into the relative performance of health systems measured in equity terms.[3]

These valuable works, however, are far too infrequent, and fail to provide the in-depth understanding of approaches in different countries that contribute to differential performance, and help health policy officials learn from the experiences of other countries. One of the challenges private foundations such as the King's Fund in the UK and The Commonwealth Fund in the USA face is how to foster this type of comparative research and translate the research into a form useful to health policy opinion formers.

Current context

Public policy debates of social security in general, and health care in particular, are occurring in most industrialised nations. Each country is struggling with the desire for change, and experimenting with innovations in health system financing and/or delivery of health care services. While the driving forces in each country differ, underlying this re-examination is a concern with the level of economic and budgetary resources devoted to health care, and political pressures to reduce public spending and taxes.

Several possible explanations account for this 'taxpayer revolt':

- International competition – the reduction of trade barriers, openness of economies to international competition, growth of multi-national firms, and emerging markets in Asia and Latin America make it difficult to tax corporations or impose labour costs on employers. If the cost of producing a product is too high in one country, operations can be shifted elsewhere.
- Stagnation of real wages – many of these same economic forces have contributed to a weakened trade union movement, slow-down in real wage increases and/or high unemployment. Failure of real incomes to grow or growing income inequality creates divisions among population groups, reduces national unity and a sense of 'being in this together,' and diminishes a commitment to equity and altruism.
- Perception of governmental inefficiency and unresponsiveness – the ideology that private spending is preferable to governmental spending, or individual responsibility is preferable to collective responsibility, is spurred by a perception that government programmes are subject to waste and resistant to innovation. In health care, there is a further concern that governmental systems of financing and/or delivering health services make health care unresponsive to patients. Health care decisions reflect the political or professional preferences of administrators, doctors and health care workers, not patients.

While these and other factors undoubtedly vary in their significance in different countries and at different points of time, they do undergird the increasing popularity of providing patients with greater choices in health care, whether through capitated managed care plans as in the USA, or other systems of decentralised budgeting or competition about public systems of care. Letting patients 'vote with their voucher' by giving them choices among health delivery organisations is believed to foster both micro-efficiency and greater consumer responsiveness.[4]

Equity and US health policy

The current US health policy debate provides a window on this broader trend. The US health system is certainly an outlier among major industrialised nations.[5] It has no universal system of health care coverage, with the result that 15 per cent of the population are uninsured. It spends more on health care as a percentage of Gross Domestic Product than any other country. Public financing of health care is limited to care for the elderly (age 65 and over) and certain groups of disabled or low-income populations; governmental outlays account for 40 per cent of US health spending – compared with 80–90 per cent in most industrialised nations.[6] As a system it has serious inequalities in access to care based on income, ability to pay, health status and insurance status. It is characterised by private market competition among both fee-for-service health care providers and managed care plans paid a capitated rate for the care of an enrolled population. For all its innovation and emphasis on private market competition, the USA spends far more while achieving less in the way of health outcomes for its population than any other country.

This is not held up as a model or even a cautionary tale. Rather the forces that are currently shaping the US health policy debate bear striking similarity to forces in other countries and may presage future trends elsewhere. The following description of the system outlines some of the major issues.

Uninsured in the USA

Today 40 million Americans are without any form of health insurance coverage, up from 32 million in 1988.[7] The proportion of Americans who are uninsured has grown steadily: 17.4 per cent of all Americans under age 65 were uninsured in 1995, compared with 15.2 per cent in 1988. Since Americans move on and off of coverage depending on their employment and eligibility for public programmes, one-fourth are uninsured over a two-year period of time.[8]

Most uninsured people have modest incomes, and the vast majority are in families headed by workers. Twenty-eight per cent of the uninsured have incomes below the poverty level, and another 32 per cent are near-poor (between poverty and twice poverty).[9] Eighty-five per cent of uninsured children and adults are in families where the family head works full or part time. While there are many reasons why people are uninsured – related to health status, unemployment, or age – the inescapable fact is that low income is the predominant risk factor. Americans are uninsured because they cannot afford health insurance coverage, and, if working, their employer does not pay for coverage.

Not surprisingly, minority ethnic Americans are hardest hit. Hispanic and Asian Americans are more likely to have jobs in the retail trade, service and agricultural sectors that do not provide health insurance benefits, and are at greatest risk of being uninsured. Thirty-five per cent of Hispanic Americans are uninsured, as are 22 per cent of African Americans.[10] Uninsurance rates are also high among Asian Americans: 23 per cent of Asian Americans are uninsured, including 38 per cent of Korean Americans.[11]

Since health insurance coverage is linked to employment, those outside the labour force (e.g. unemployed, early retirees and disabled people) are also at high risk of being uninsured. One-fourth of all non-working adults under age 65 are uninsured. Public programmes cover those with long-term disability, but only after a two-year waiting period in the case of Medicare (see below), and after meeting stringent income and asset eligibility requirements in the case of Medicaid (see below). Half of those unemployed are either currently uninsured or have been uninsured at some time in the last two years.[12]

Perhaps the most seriously at risk are those between the ages of 55 and 64. While older adults are less likely than younger people to be uninsured, they are more likely to be in fair or poor health, to face high individual health insurance premiums when coverage is available at all, and to risk financial hardship if they incur major medical expenses. Two-and-a-half million Americans between the ages of 55 and 64 are uninsured, and almost one million are doubly vulnerable – they are in fair or poor health and have no health insurance coverage.[13] Poor, older adults are particularly at risk: 28 per cent of adults aged 58 to 63 with poverty incomes are uninsured, compared with 5 per cent of those with incomes above twice poverty.[14]

The consequences of being uninsured include failure to get preventive care, inadequate maintenance of chronic conditions and adverse health outcomes. Those who are uninsured are less likely to receive needed medical care and more likely to postpone care and wait until medical needs become an emergency. Thirty-four per cent of those uninsured report failure to receive needed care during the year, and 71 per cent postpone needed care.[15]

This failure to receive proper care takes an economic toll in terms of preventable hospitalisation, disability and mortality.[16] It also inflicts financial hardships on those who are sick, and increases emotional stress on families during a time of serious illness. For society as a whole, the preventable disease and poor health result in high 'indirect costs' as well, owing to lost work days, lowered productivity and premature deaths. Estimated indirect costs of chronic disease came to $234 billion, with 4.5 million years of productivity lost owing to sick days and another 24 million years lost owing to premature death.[17]

Productivity is reduced, as workers are unable to work either because of their own illness or the necessity of caring for sick family members. Health is an extremely important determinant of early exit from the labour force, and accounts for almost all of the 2:1 ratio of black versus white middle-aged men out of the workforce.[18] Women, particularly, feel the brunt of caring for a disabled child, spouse, or parent, and are often unable to work themselves because of this care-giving responsibility.[19]

Despite a compelling case on equity and economic grounds, US policy efforts to expand coverage to the uninsured have been thwarted throughout the 20th century. In the last 20 years, Presidents Carter and Clinton proposed universal health insurance plans that were defeated. While the explanations for this failure were many, financing is a major barrier. Since those who are uninsured have modest incomes, redistribution of income through taxation or other means is required to finance expanded coverage for the 15 per cent of the population without coverage. Opposition by small business to contributing toward health insurance costs for workers was especially intense. In addition, those who currently provide health insurance or health services have a strong vested interest in opposing any plan that would reallocate resources, leading to difficult political battles.

In the aftermath of the most recent failure of the Clinton health reform plan, the policy debate has focused on more modest incremental expansion of health insurance coverage for those perceived at greatest vulnerability – especially children in low-income families. Even in this debate, however, sharp divisions have erupted over whether to expand existing public insurance programmes (specifically Medicaid), provide subsidies or vouchers for the purchase of private insurance, or to give state governments block grants to design their own children's health programmes.

Medicaid

The federal-state Medicaid programme is a major source of health insurance for low-income Americans. Medicaid covers 37 million people – more than one in eight Americans – including low-income children, parents (mostly mothers), disabled, and elderly people. Without Medicaid, almost half of the poor and near-poor population would be uninsured. Indeed, if low-income women succeed in working their way off of welfare and as a consequence are no longer eligible for Medicaid, they are likely to become uninsured: almost two-thirds (63 per cent) of women leaving Medicaid are uninsured.[20]

Medicaid has been particularly important in recent years in offsetting some of the decline in employer-based insurance. More than 10 million people, mostly low-income mothers and children, were added to Medicaid coverage over the last ten years through legislative changes that set federal income eligibility standards for children and pregnant women tied to the federal poverty level. Today, among poor families, 76 per cent of infants are covered by Medicaid, as are 72 per cent of children aged one to five, and 64 per cent of children aged 6–12.[21] Under current law, Medicaid coverage of poor children aged 13–18 will be fully phased in by the year 2002.

Medicaid has markedly improved access to health care and served as a crucial safety net for the nation's most vulnerable populations, caring for individuals who would otherwise have few options available to meet their health needs.[22] Gains in access to care for significant numbers of low-income people have translated into important health gains.[23] Although it is difficult to isolate the independent contribution of improved coverage, since 1965, when Medicaid was introduced, maternal mortality has fallen by three-quarters and infant mortality has halved. Age-adjusted death rates are down substantially for leading causes of death amenable to improved medical care. Life expectancy at birth has increased by six years; almost half these gains can be attributed to improved medical care.[24]

Medicaid, however, is currently undergoing strain. The expansion of coverage, increased disability and rise in conditions such as HIV have placed fiscal pressure on federal and state budgets. States have turned to managed care as a way of controlling costs. In a short period of time, one-third of Medicaid beneficiaries have been enrolled in managed care plans, often with inadequate quality controls or standards. Some states are planning to enrol their entire Medicaid population – not just mothers and children but those who are seriously disabled and frail. This is largely uncharted territory, and how well managed care plans that have little experience providing specialised services to low-income disabled populations will perform is an unanswered question.

Medicare

Medicare is the major source of basic health insurance for the nation's 38 million elderly and disabled people. Particularly striking has been the programme's success in improving access to care for low income and minority ethnic elderly Americans. Racial disparities in care for elderly Americans have largely been eliminated and Medicare was instrumental in spurring the desegregation of medical facilities when it was enacted in 1965. Medicare has also contributed to the development of research and innovation, through its funding of medical education and more generous allowances for teaching hospitals.

Despite its success, however, Medicare benefits have remained relatively modest. It covers only 45 per cent of the health care expenses of older people, both because it requires substantial cost-sharing (e.g. $760 deductible for hospital care in 1997 and 20 per cent co-insurance for physician services) and because it does not cover such services as prescription drugs, dental care and long-term care. Today, older Americans pay 21 per cent of their own incomes for health care, and low-income elderly people even with Medicaid supplemental coverage devote 30 per cent of their incomes to health care expenses.[25]

Given current budgetary pressures, however, the prospects for improving benefits are dim. The rising cost of health care generally, as well as the increase in life expectancy and growing numbers of older people are causing the programme cost to increase at a 8–9 per cent annual rate at a time when budget pressures are trying to contain the growth in the federal budget to a 4–5 per cent rate of increase. Various proposals have been advanced to curtail spending, including reductions in provider payment rates and health maintenance organisation (HMO) premiums, overall expenditure capping, expansion of enrolment in managed care plans, substitution of current benefits for a fixed voucher or medical savings account combined with catastrophic coverage, and higher beneficiary financial contributions.

Even without legislative changes, increasing numbers of Medicare beneficiaries are enrolling in managed care plans. Currently, 14 per cent of all Medicare beneficiaries are enrolled in HMOs, but enrolment is growing rapidly.[26] The Congressional Budget Office estimates that Medicare HMO enrolment will reach 35 per cent by the year 2007.[27] Beneficiary experience to date seems mixed. There is some evidence that relatively healthier beneficiaries are more likely to enrol in HMOs than are sicker beneficiaries.[28] Among those joining, Medicare managed-care beneficiaries are more likely to be found at both ends of the spectrum, either very satisfied or very dissatisfied with their care, than are those continuing under traditional Medicare coverage.[29] Medicare beneficiaries enrolled in HMOs are less likely to be very satisfied or confident in their doctors' care and skills than those in traditional Medicare, yet more are satisfied with coverage of costs.[30] The attraction, however, is that managed care plans offer comprehensive benefits, often with lower out-of-pocket costs to Medicare beneficiaries, and reduce the hassle of filing claims.

Proposals to substitute traditional Medicare coverage for vouchers or medical savings account would further segment the Medicare population into different groups. It seems likely that only the relatively well-to-do and healthy would be attracted to medical savings accounts combined with catastrophic health insurance coverage that leaves them financially responsible for health expenses of $5,000 or more per year. Since 75 per cent of Medicare beneficiaries have incomes under $25,000, this financial liability is unlikely to be either attractive or sound for the bulk of beneficiaries.

Elements of means-testing surfaced in the 1997 budget debate. The US Senate supported an income-related premium that would phase out subsidies for Medicare physician and other ambulatory care services for higher-income beneficiaries (individuals with incomes above $100,000 and couples with incomes above $125,000), but this proposal was not included in the final legislation. Some modest increases in premium subsidies for those with incomes below 150 per cent of the federal poverty level were added (below $10,500 for a single elderly person).

These proposals share the limitation that they undermine the social insurance nature of Medicare where those who are healthy cross-subsidise those who are sick, and those who are well-to-do pay more into the system than those who are of modest means. Furthermore, they increase the uncertainty of out-of-pocket medical expenses in old age, and threaten to undermine the gains in economic security achieved by older people in the last 30 years.

Employer coverage

The principal way in which most Americans receive health insurance coverage is through their place of employment. Today 72 per cent of the employed workforce has employer health insurance coverage from their own employer or a spouse's employer.[31] Employer-provided health insurance, however, has begun to decline as a source of coverage. By 1995, only 64 per cent of the under-65 population (including children and non-working adults) had employer-sponsored insurance, down from 69 per cent in 1988. This decline is largely due to the changing nature of where people work and a decline in the share of premium paid by employers, especially for coverage of spouses and children.[32] As jobs have moved out of manufacturing, workers have moved away from industries with relatively generous sponsorship of family coverage to industries less likely to provide health insurance at all, and with much less generous premium coverage. Younger workers with children, in particular, are more likely to be working in the service sector where health benefits are less common.

Retiree health coverage is eroding even more rapidly than worker coverage. The proportion of retirees ages 55 and over currently receiving health benefits from their prior employer declined from 44 per cent to 34 per cent in the period 1988–1994.[33] The decline in coverage results from a combination of factors, including lower coverage of workers during their working years (and thus no option of retiree coverage), reduction in offering retiree coverage, and increasing share of premium shifted to retirees. For lower-income older adults without employer coverage, the cost of insurance is high: half of those with incomes below 200 per cent of poverty pay more than 15 per cent of their family income just for health insurance premiums.[34]

Managed care and employer coverage

The erosion of employer-based coverage has affected not only the numbers of workers and retirees with coverage, but the quality of coverage as well. Workers have been faced with an increasing premium cost, higher deductibles, and out-of-pocket costs. The major shift, however, has been the decline in traditional health insurance coverage, which gave working families the option of selecting any doctor or health care provider of their choice. Today, 80 per cent of workers in medium- and large-size firms enrol in managed care plans which require families to seek care from a defined set of doctors and other health care providers.[35] Only 40 per cent of adults in working families are offered more than one plan by their employer.[36] When workers do have a choice of a traditional health insurance plan, they often must pay a substantially higher premium for this option. As a result, lower-wage workers are much more likely to opt for managed care coverage.

The implications of managed care for quality of care are still not clear. The rapid evolution of the industry, with new and changing forms of organisation, has outpaced research on performance. The basic concerns about quality come from the incentives inherent in a capitated form of payment to managed care plans. Plans receive the same revenues, regardless of the quantity and quality of health services provided to enrolled beneficiaries. Profits are higher, therefore, when costs are lower – either from increased efficiency or lower quality and limited services. In a world of perfect information and many choices, market forces could lead to the financial failure of low-quality inferior plans. However, information is quite limited, techniques for measuring quality and performance are rudimentary, choices are few, and both employers as purchasers and managed care plans have major incentives to reduce costs regardless of the consequences for quality.

Quality of care may be affected in numerous ways. By linking where patients go for care to their particular insurance coverage, any change in plan often requires changing doctor, disrupting the continuity of care.[37] A 1997 Kaiser/Commonwealth Health Insurance Survey found that 31 per cent of adults in working families changed health plans in the last two years, and that for two-fifths this required changing doctor.[38] Studies show that patients benefit from having a long-term ongoing relationship with the same doctor.[39] Studies of managed care enrollees also identify problems with access to needed specialist care, difficulty in obtaining appointments, and lower-quality care.[40] Most troubling is recent evidence that managed care works less well for low-income patients, leading to restricted access to services and poorer health outcomes.[41] There may also be system-wide effects of managed care. Studies indicate that managed care plans are steering patients away from academic health centres with advanced teaching hospitals; while more costly such institutions play a critical role in the testing and diffusion of the latest medical advances.[42]

Market incentives

Market incentives are transforming the US health care system. Large-scale purchasers, mostly capitated managed care plans, are succeeding in negotiating price discounts from doctors and hospitals – in a largely oversupplied health care industry. Assuring genuine competition under multiple systems of care has promise for making health care more affordable, promoting efficiency and provision of appropriate care, and imposes much needed restraints on health care costs.

However, the reality of the evolution of managed care raises concerns. Half of all HMO enrollees – the primary form of managed care – are in eight large managed care plans. The managed-care industry has shifted in a relatively short period of time from a non-profit industry to a for-profit industry, with publicly traded plans.[43]

The incentives in fee-for-service care are to provide too many services at too high cost. The incentives in managed care are to provide too few services at too low quality. Effective competition between both traditional fee-for-service coverage and managed care at least holds the promise of avoiding the extreme of either system. However, increasingly in employer plans and in Medicaid, the only option available is a managed care plan. Whether limited competition among large managed care plans motivated primarily by profit will live up to the desire for efficient and responsive care remains to be seen.

Quality and performance standards

Choice is only meaningful, in any event, if the systems of care on offer meet quality and performance standards, and if information on quality and performance is collected and disseminated to all parties. The USA has not developed such standards or information as part of deliberate public policy. Rather, driven by employers' concerns, a private non-profit organisation was established to accredit managed care plans and provide uniform data on quality indicators. The National Committee for Quality Assurance (NCQA) is the major non-profit accrediting body for managed care plans. It has begun, through its Health Employer Data Information System (HEDIS 3.0), to assemble quality and performance indicators on plans. However, currently only about half of managed care plans seek accreditation and not all voluntarily supply HEDIS data. Requiring all managed care plans to meet minimum quality standards, submit standardised data on quality and performance, and make such data available to the public is a minimum safeguard to ensure effective competition and quality.

Other safeguards for which public policy is needed are recourse if patients are denied needed care or if doctors are not able to provide care which they believe to be in the best interest of patients. Patients should have the right to appeal against denials of services external to the plan and the right to disenrol from plans that are not meeting their needs. Physicians should have the right to act as advocates for their patients and to ensure that they have access to needed specialty care.

A multi-tiered health system

The implications of the market-driven fragmented US health care system are further movement away from equity in health care, and increased tiering of the health system. Those fortunate enough to work for larger firms with generous health benefits and choices of plans, and to have sufficient incomes and information to pick higher- quality coverage may continue to receive high-quality health care when needed. At the other extreme, a growing number of Americans (one-sixth of those under age 65) are without any health insurance coverage, and their access to sources of free care is increasingly limited by competition among health care providers to lower costs. Medicaid beneficiaries will increasingly be required to enrol in managed care plans, with as yet unknown consequences for quality of care but in an environment where the major priority is controlling costs. Lower-income workers who are fortunate enough to have employer-provided coverage still face financial burdens from required premium contributions and out-of-pocket costs, or may be required to enrol in managed care plans which impose barriers to needed care. Medicare beneficiaries currently have choices of selecting their own doctor or enrolling in a qualified managed care plan with at least minimum quality requirements, but mounting fiscal pressures may also segment beneficiaries into different arrangements with different consequences for access and quality.

All of these trends are the result of the unique US system of financing health care in different ways for different population groups, rather than a single universal system available to all. It is in striking contrast to health systems in other industrialised nations that provide comprehensive benefits, with little or no out-of-pocket costs, cover the elderly and the non-elderly alike, and devote a much lower percentage of their national economic resources to health care. To argue that the USA is unable to afford comprehensive coverage for all when all other major industrialised nations do so is untenable. Rather it is a reflection of policy choices that shape the US health system – choices that can be changed so that economic prosperity in the USA can be deployed to ensure that all Americans have access to needed health care and that the health and productivity of Americans are not undermined by inadequate prevention and treatment of health conditions.

Sharing prosperity

As international competition forces all major industrialised nations to restructure their economies and their industries to become more efficient, a resurgence of economic growth can be expected. The challenge facing industrialised nations as they move into the next century is how to share this economic prosperity equitably among their citizens. Social programmes and a safety net to ensure access to health care and a decent living standard are particularly of concern. National health policy that promotes health security should have the following basic components:

- commitment to financing health care for all;
- incremental change to improve efficiency and equity, including defining relative roles for government and private organisations and their interaction;
- appropriate use of choices for patients and market forces to promote efficiency and responsiveness;
- establishment and enforcement of uniform quality standards.

While each country will need to find its own way, there is much to be gained by pooling the shared experiences of major health systems as they grapple with understanding the options available and the consequences for equity and efficiency.[44] International examination will be critical and will help put each country's unique situation in the context of common concerns. Fortunately, a growing body of trained researchers with the tools and data to facilitate such research provide a unique opportunity to capitalise on the 'natural experiments' taking place around the world. The end result should be growing international co-operation and collaboration dedicated to achieving the goal of health for all people.

References
1. Maxwell RJ. *Health and wealth: an international study of health care spending.* Lexington (Mass.): Lexington Press, 1981.
2. Schieber GJ, Poullier J-P, Greenwald LM. Health systems performance in OECD countries, 1980–1992. *Health Affairs* 1994; Fall, pp. 100–12.

3. Van Doorslaer E, Wagstaff A, Rutten F. *Equity in the finance and delivery of health care: an international perspective.* Oxford: Oxford University Press, 1993.
4. Chernichovsky D. Health system reforms in industrialized democracies: an emerging paradigm. *Health Affairs* 1995; 73(3):339–72.

5. Davis K. Equity and health care policy: the American experience. In: Van Doorslaer E, Wagstaff A, Rutten F (eds). *Equity in the finance and delivery of health care: an international perspective.* Oxford: Oxford University Press, 1993.
6. *Health Care Financing Review Annual Supplement,* 1989.
7. Fronstin P. *Sources of health insurance and characteristics of the uninsured: analysis of the March 1996 current population survey.* Employee Benefit Research Institute Issue Brief No. 179, November 1996.
8. Bennefield RL. *Who loses coverage for how long? Dynamics of economic well being: health insurance, 1992 to 1994.* Survey of Income and Program Participation, US Department of Commerce, May 1996.
9. See 7.
10. See 7.
11. Collins KS. Minority health. *Bulletin of the New York Academy of Medicine* 1995; Winter Supplement, based on: The Commonwealth Fund. *Comparative minority health survey of Whites, African Americans, Hispanics, and Asian Americans.* 1994
12. Davis K, Rowland D, Altman D, Collins KS, Morris C. Health insurance: the size and shape of the problem. *Inquiry* 1995; 32(2):196–203.
13. Davis K. *Uninsured older adults: the need for a Medicare buy-in option.* Testimony before the Committee on Ways and Means, Subcommittee on Health, June 12, 1990.
14. Loprest P, Uccello C. *Uninsured older adults: implications for changing Medicare eligibility age.* The Commonwealth Fund, January 1997.
15. See 12.
16. Hoffman C, Rice D, Sung H-Y. Persons with chronic conditions. Their prevalence and costs. *The Journal of the American Medical Association* 1996; 276(18): 1473–9.
17. See 16.
18. Bound J, Schoenbaum M, Waidmann T. *Race differences in labor force attachment and disability status.* National Bureau of Economic Research, Working Paper No. 5536, November 1996.
19. Wolfe BL, Hill SC. The effect of health on the work effort of single mothers. *Journal of Human Resources* 1994; 30 (1).
20. Short PF. *Medicaid's role in insuring low-income women.* The Commonwealth Fund, May 1996.
21. See 7.

22. Schoen C, Lyons B, Rowland D, Davis K, Puleo E. Insurance matters for low-income adults: results from the Kaiser/Commonwealth Five State Low-Income Survey. *Health Affairs* 1997; September/October 16(5): 163–71.

23. Rowland D. Lessons from the Medicaid experience. In: Ginzberg E (ed). *Critical issues in US health reform*. Boulder (CO): Westview Press, 1994, pp. 190–207.

24. Bunker JP, Frazier HS, Mosteller F. Improving health: measuring effects of medical care. *Milbank Memorial Fund Quarterly* 1994; 72(2).

25. Moon M, Crystal K, Pounder L. *Protecting low income Medicare beneficiaries*. The Commonwealth Fund, December 1996.

26. Health Care Financing Administration. *Profiles of Medicare*. 1996.

27. Congressional Budget Office, January 1997.

28. Physician Payment Review Commission. Risk selection and risk adjustment in Medicare. In: *Annual Report to Congress*. Washington DC, 1996.

29. See 26.

30. Adler G. Medicare beneficiaries rate their medical care: new data from the MCBS. *Health Care Financing Review* 1995; 16(4):175–87.

31. See 7.

32. Thorpe KE. *What accounts for the reduction in employer-sponsored insurance: the role of employment shifts, Medicaid, and family structure*. Draft report to The Commonwealth Fund, Fall 1996.

33. US Department of Labor. *Retirement benefits of American workers: new findings from the September 1994 Current Population Survey*, September 1995.

34. See 14.

35. KPMG Peat Marwick. *Health benefits in 1997: executive summary*. Arlington (Va): KPMG Peat Marwick, June 1997.

36. Davis K. *Managed care, choice, and patient satisfaction*. Testimony before the President's Advisory Commission on Consumer Protection and Quality in the Health Care Industry, June 25, 1997.

37. Davis K, Collins KS, Schoen C, Morris C. Choice matters: enrollees' views of their health plans. *Health Affairs* 1995; 14, Summer.

38. See 22.

39. Weiss Lj, Blustein J. Faithful patients: the effect of long-term physician-patient relationships on the elderly's use and costs of care. *American Journal of Public Health* 1996; 86, December.

40. See 12.

41. Ware J *et al*. Differences in 4-year health outcomes for elderly and poor, chronically ill patients treated in HMO and fee-for-service systems: results from the medical outcomes study. *Journal of the American Medical Association* 1996; 276(13):1039–47.

42. Hadley J, Gaskin DJ. *Policy brief: preliminary evidence on the impact of HMO market enrollment on academic health center hospitals.* Institute for Health Care Research and Policy, Georgetown University Medical Center, 1995; Meyer GS, Blumenthal D. TennCare and academic medical centers: the lessons from Tennessee. *Journal of the American Medical Association* 1996; 276(9):672–6.

43. Gabel J. Ten ways HMOs have changed during the 1990s. *Health Affairs* 1996; May/June, pp. 134–5.

44. Davis K. What Americans can learn from Europeans. *Health Care Financing Review Annual Supplement* 1989; pp. 104–5.

Health care reform: a European perspective

David J. Hunter
Professor of Health Policy & Management,
Nuffield Institute for Health

Health care reform has become a major industry worldwide for various reasons, including a shared concern among governments to contain costs and increase efficiency.[1] In many countries the policy proposals to tackle these and other systemic problems have been quite radical, while their implementation and impact, in marked contrast, have been piecemeal and often, for all the rhetoric surrounding them, far less radical. Some countries have opted for 'big bang' reform, while others have adopted an incremental approach. Despite evidence of a convergence when it comes to diagnosing the ailments that have long troubled health care systems, the implementation of reforms, which themselves may appear to converge, occurs in very different contexts with their own traditions and cultural traits.

The pathology of health care reform is well displayed within a European context where virtually every manifestation of the phenomenon is in evidence somewhere to some degree. This is especially the case when the experience of the countries of central and eastern Europe and the commonwealth of independent states (CIS) is reviewed. In these countries health care reform, where it has taken off, has been of a fundamental root-and-branch nature that has often been different in kind from health care systems in countries in western and northern Europe.[2]

The purpose of this essay is to review the European experience of health care reform in general terms, drawing out key themes while concentrating in particular on the 'convergence versus divergence' debate and, arising from this, what Britain can learn from, and/or contribute to, health care reform at a European level. Although much is made in the academic and policy analysis literature of the value and virtues of lesson-learning across countries facing shared problems and adopting similar solutions, in reality governments seem to prefer operating in isolation and to ignore the lessons others may have to offer. Paradoxically, however, though governments may not actively indulge in lesson-learning, they are in the fashion business when it comes to policy-making and structural reorganisation in health care as elsewhere. Here, the experiences of other countries, regardless of whether they are good or bad, become all-important. So it was in the case of the British National Health Service changes introduced in 1991 when the Government found itself to be a market leader in health care reform with countries, in Europe and elsewhere, looking to developments such as hospital trusts, GP fundholding and the purchaser/provider separation as ones they might usefully mimic.[3] Significantly, this was at a time when there was very little hard evidence available as to whether these changes were desirable and were achieving the objectives for which they were intended.[4,5] As a WHO review of strategies for reforming health care in Europe noted, 'in certain instances, the debate has been driven by ideology and rhetoric more than by evidence that substantiates anticipated benefits'.[3] But in the high fashion of health care reform where market principles and notions of competition and a 'contract culture' were well to the fore, evidence as to their effectiveness was somehow less important than being seen to be talking the same language and implementing the same kinds of changes, albeit adapted to distinctive national settings.

The meaning of health care reform in Europe

A dilemma when we speak of health care reform concerns what precisely we mean by it. What, for instance, distinguishes health care reform from the myriad daily changes that are part of every health care system? Is it a 'big bang' change of the type for which the UK achieved a certain reputation or notoriety?[6] Or is it incremental change of the kind evident in The Netherlands? Or is it perhaps a mix of the two as seems to be the case in at least some of the Nordic countries?

It is probably reasonable to say that when we speak of health care reform we are referring to a period which began in the 1980s/early 1990s when many European governments began to subject their health care systems to searching scrutiny and, in some cases, to major change of a nature and on a scale not hitherto witnessed. Virtually all these countries remain in a process of transition, although, in the case of countries like the UK which have recently experienced a change of government, it is far from clear what the destination is or even what this transitional state entails. If there is a common theme shared by countries, it is one of change within change – systems in a state of almost continuous transformation where there is no blueprint and where often the endpoint of all this intensive activity is unclear or ill defined. In these circumstances, it appears as if the process of change is itself an outcome if not *the* outcome.

Of course, health care reform means different things to different groups. Clearly, it means one thing to its architects. But does it mean the same to doctors and other practitioners who may have been (and often remain) extremely critical of the reforms? And what about the public who for the most part probably do not understand the changes but who may, all the same, feel troubled by them or even become cynical about their true purpose and the real intentions of reformers whose soothing blandishments and actions they intrinsically distrust? It is fair to say that across European health care systems, reform is a highly contentious issue among key stakeholders. Not surprisingly, it is replete with paradox, ambiguity and contradiction.

Despite its technocratic pretensions and perception that it is informed by a rational conception of policy-making, in practice health care reform is no such thing. For all the fashionable management-speak, it is an intensely political activity. Health policy is generally driven by a mix of ideology, fashion and pragmatism and while the UK may be a leading exponent of the art, other European countries either already display or have adopted a similar stance.[7] It certainly cannot be argued that health care reform has been based on sound evidence or tested models that have been piloted and evaluated because that has not happened either in this country or elsewhere in Europe.[8,9] Indeed, in the UK at least, one senior minister made a virtue out of not letting academic researchers loose on the changes because, in his view, that would probably have scuppered the changes and allowed their opponents to undermine them. Moreover, despite the welcome introduction of an NHS R&D strategy in the UK (one of the more useful and possibly lasting changes introduced in 1991), it did not at the outset devote its attention or resources to evaluating the health care changes. Even if it had, it is doubtful whether ministers would have heeded its findings or recommendations.

The present Labour Government has committed itself to proceeding on the basis of pilots and experiments which will be evaluated, with only those shown to be effective or worthwhile being rolled out nationally. However, already changes are under way in respect of trust, and possibly health authority, mergers for which the evidence base in the critical areas of cost savings and improved quality of service is lacking. For all their good intentions governments find it difficult to operate according to the tenets of evidence-based policy-making. They also find it difficult to avoid tinkering with the structure of health care systems, despite the concerns that such actions often achieve little and divert attention and resources from the important issues. As Robert Maxwell has asked: 'What is the real problem to which organisational change has been the symptomatic response rather than the solution?'[10] Simply put, the real problem is the attempt to square the circle of rising expectations within tight fiscal constraints. In Maxwell's well-chosen words, 'It is a wicked rather than a tame problem in the sense that it has no neat or permanent solution'.[10]

The position elsewhere in Europe is, if anything, even more problematic in this respect. Sweden is a possible exception where health care reform has proceeded incrementally and where attempts have been made to undertake evaluation of some aspects of the changes. Possibly, Sweden's devolved system of health care which is under local political control encourages such an approach. It certainly rules out the imposition by central government of a uniform philosophy and package of changes in contrast to the experience of the UK. It is often remarked that the UK is the most centralised state in Europe, and there is no doubt that this fact enabled central government to push through its NHS reforms with remarkable speed and uniformity across the country. With devolution to Scotland and Wales now a certainty, future policy-making in areas like health will not remain so centralised. It is likely, too, that England will not escape pressure from at least some of its regions to devolve power to regional assemblies at some future date.

But should we be surprised to discover that policy is not based on evidence or that what exists is flawed or incomplete and therefore unreliable? Not really. Politicians, for quite understandable reasons, do not wish to be diverted from their chosen course of action by evidence which may challenge their cherished assumptions or contradict their dearly held beliefs. On this point, there is little distinguishing policy-makers across Europe. This observation has implications for the apparent desire, frequently voiced, to share and learn from the experiences of others.

Most European countries, then, have been (and still are) actively engaged in what can only be termed natural experiments (which may be huge and ambitious or small and modest) when it comes to the reform of their health care systems. 'Learning by doing' is a term often employed to describe this process. But, as has been suggested, while there is plenty of doing in evidence, the learning may be rather less obvious. This observation is picked up by Figueras *et al.* who argue that while the UK NHS reforms have had a major if not decisive influence on the content of health care reforms in several countries both in western and eastern Europe, 'there is ... surprisingly little evidence on the actual effectiveness of some reform policies not only in those countries on the receiving end but also in countries championing these policies'.[9](p.1) They cite one Scandinavian commentator who has argued that there is a general 'reformitis' at large throughout Europe with little empirical evidence 'ex ante' and with even less 'ex post' evaluation to justify such an outbreak of policy change. In such a situation there is a risk that health care systems will simultaneously undergo change and no change. Donald Schön has termed this phenomenon 'dynamics without change'.[11]

Assessing the European experience: convergence versus divergence

Despite the considerable difficulties, it is nevertheless possible to make some assessment of developments in health care systems in recent years across Europe. Some of the problems diagnosed, and seemingly common to all countries or at any rate to a significant number of them, have been addressed and similar solutions found albeit within very different political, social, economic and cultural parameters and contexts. But the convergence theme should not be overstated. There exists considerable diversity across Europe in respect of culture, values and levels of wealth and development. Reform strategies which work in one country cannot simply be exported to other countries without adaptation. It is therefore incorrect to assert that common policy strategies are appropriate or applicable across Europe. In this respect, the convergence thesis (see below) may have overplayed specific reform techniques and instruments at the expense of the purpose to which they are put. The politics of health care reform cannot be ignored. They suggest the need for a flexible response.

In considering health care reform in Europe it is useful to cite two theoretical approaches: the convergence hypothesis, and the combined universalistic and particularistic hypothesis. The first of these holds that countries are converging both in the nature of the problems they face and in the solutions selected to tackle them. The second hypothesis takes a rather more subtle view of the evolution and dynamics of health care reform across countries and holds that while a degree of convergence is present, particularly when it comes to the diagnosis of problems, the selection and application of solutions, even where they appear common, tends to be tailored or customised to the prevailing political, social, economic and cultural conditions evident in a particular country. This second hypothesis more accurately captures the reality of health care reform. It also happens to be supported by WHO's overview of the health care reform experience in Europe. As its report states:

> Currently across Europe, different countries are in different stages of [the reform] cycle. Several western European countries are setting out on major experiments. Conversely, in the countries of northern Europe that began their reforms the earliest, there is now substantial movement back from the radical position – market-oriented incentives – closer to the original position of publicly planned co-ordination and co-operation. Similarly, in some CIS countries, a tendency can be seen to compare the current extremely difficult conditions with the health systems of the former Soviet period – which at least functioned – and to hesitate about how to proceed.[3] (p.265)

In summarising the changes in health care systems since the 1970s, Ham[12] has usefully grouped these into three phases (see Box 1). In keeping with the diversity noted above, not all these themes and topics have been evident in European countries to the same degree

Box 1   Phases in health care reform

Phase one	Late 1970s/early 1980s
Theme:	Cost containment at macro-level
Policy instruments:	Prospective global budgets for hospitals
	Controls on hospital building
	Controls on acquisition of medical equipment
	Limits on doctors' fees and incomes
	Restrictions on numbers in training
Phase two	Late 1980s/early 1990s
Theme:	Micro-efficiency and responsiveness to users
Policy instruments:	Market-like mechanisms
	Management reforms
	Budgetary incentives
Phase three	Late 1990s
Theme:	Rationing and priority setting
Policy instruments:	Public health
	Primary care
	Managed care
	Health technology assessment
	Evidence-based medicine

Source: Ham[12]

or simultaneously, but it is reasonable to maintain that they have all been on the policy agendas in these countries at one time or another.

Health care reform in Europe has been characterised by countries seeking to move away from command and control, planned/managed systems of health care to those which place an emphasis on markets and competition in the belief, and it is no more than that, that their adoption will increase efficiency and reduce the 'burden' on public spending. Of course, such preoccupations are not confined

A	B	C	D
Command and control	Planned/ managed	Regulated	Neo-classical free markets
North, South, West ⟶		Central and East/FSU ⟶	

Figure 1 Health care reform in Europe

to Europe being core components of the globalisation of economic policy with its dogma about the disutilities of public spending. The different models of health care reform are mapped on a continuum set out in Figure 1. Most countries in the West, North and South of Europe have sought to move from Mode A to somewhere around B and C. A few central and eastern European countries have sought to move to Mode D, which most closely resembles the US 'non-system' of health care and is based on a much reduced role for public funding and public provision. But, as noted above, these shifts are rarely stable but tend to be dynamic and cyclical. Countries can (and do) move back and forth along the continuum at different stages in their development and perception of what action it is proper to take.

When it comes to countries reforming their health care systems, there are two scenarios. In the first scenario, all health care financing and most service delivery remain public goods plus hybrid delivery models which may be a mix of public and private (both for profit and not for profit). In this scenario, the financing of health care is public in origin either through taxation or through some form of social insurance scheme, while the provision may be public, private or a mix of public and private inputs. In the second scenario a more pluralistic perspective is adopted. Here there is fragmentation of both financing and service production into multiple competing private as well as publicly capitalised units. Health care reform in European countries has proceeded according to one or other of these scenarios. For the most part, the first scenario has been adopted in northern, western and southern Europe, while the second scenario has found favour in central and eastern Europe.

At the level of policy values and objectives these are generally shared across Europe, although they are not consistent or mutually reinforcing. In fact they can be contradictory. They include the following elements: adequate services for all, equity of access, protection of income for providers, efficiency at both macro- and micro-levels, consumer choice. The contradictions are multiple but one example will make the point. While there need not be a conflict between micro-efficiency and consumer choice, the chances are there will be. The entire history of health care reform has been a response to a series of persistent policy puzzles, including: how to ensure high quality services, the provision of health care which enhances health gain, appropriate regulation of providers, achieving equity, locating the optimal balance between public and private inputs, and the productive involvement of the public. The fact that many of these issues remain in good currency is testimony to their persistence over many years. Recent health care reform moves have resulted in some new puzzles to add to the list. These revolve around the tension between individual versus collective notions of health, individual consumer choice versus the solidarity principle which remains a strong feature across Europe, competition versus collaboration, and the vexed question of rationing or, as some prefer to call it, priority-setting.

What has Britain contributed to health care reform?

Through the efforts of the British Government itself operating principally through the Department of Health/NHS Executive, the Department for International Development (the ODA as it then was) and through the efforts of international organisations such as WHO, the World Bank and OECD as well as various international management consultancies, the NHS reforms have been widely disseminated throughout Europe and beyond. What Britain had to 'sell' or offer other countries was useful experience and thinking around an array of supply-side changes, principally at the micro-level, designed to raise the level of efficiency in health care provision. For countries confronting a surfeit of hospital beds, inefficient operating units and lacking a strong management ethos and capability, the British changes offered a model at least worthy of closer inspection. But what is particularly striking about the appeal of the British NHS reforms is the attention devoted to process issues. While the ends were not forgotten, it was the means which were a source of considerable and enduring interest. How were budgets devolved to GPs? What did contracting entail in practice? What did a contract look like? How were trusts set up and what freedoms did they enjoy? How were purchasers tooled up to perform their function? And so on. It was the details which fascinated overseas observers and because Britain had been at it longer than most and had moved more quickly from the drawing board to implementation with minimal opportunity to dilute or modify the proposed changes, the NHS experience provided a rich and valuable source of advice not only on the proposals themselves but also on their implementation and the tactics and stratagems which might be deployed.

Unlike most European countries, it is the NHS management tradition which has made the British experience particularly interesting, possibly valuable and almost certainly (within a European context) unique. The interface between management and medicine had been confronted in Britain in a way that was quite distinct from the European experience. What was especially impressive to visitors to Britain intent upon seeing the changes for themselves was the speed with which the 1991 reforms were implemented simultaneously, and more or less uniformly, across the country. To achieve this, ministers had to look to, and rely upon, managers who, after all, were their agents. Managers were ultimately accountable to the Secretary of State for Health and were therefore obliged to do their bidding. For many managers this was not seen as being in any way incompatible with their own mission, as they were perhaps the most obvious beneficiaries of the changes since they granted managers additional power, while at the same time insisting that doctors should become more accountable for their actions and more corporate in their approach to making decisions and allocating resources. For other countries rather more obviously doctor-dominated, the cult of managerialism, alien to their traditions, has been viewed with considerable interest and possibly even envy in some cases.

But there has been much interest in other possibly less obvious aspects of the changes, too. Some of these were not at the time of the 1991 reforms seen as that significant but they have subsequently moved to centre stage. The first of these is the NHS R&D strategy with its stress on knowledge-based decision-making. The evidence-based medicine movement and notions of clinical effectiveness have their origins in this initiative. Few other countries have invested in a high-profile R&D function and have looked to the UK as an exemplar in this area. With notions of managed care entering the health care reform vocabulary, the management of clinical activity is going to become a more significant issue than it currently is. Evidence-based medicine will become crucial to the success of such developments on the policy and management side. Of course there remains a long way to go in the UK before a research culture can truly be said to exist throughout the NHS. For the most part, evidence does not yet inform managers' decisions or clinical work.

The other area which has attracted considerable attention is the health strategy, *The Health of the Nation*. Introduced in 1992 almost as an afterthought following the reforms to the health care delivery system, it has never been taken entirely seriously by an NHS preoccupied with short-term financial pressures. But the health strategy, the first ever of its type in the NHS, was seen as desirable, if not essential, to provide a coherent policy framework governing the activities of the NHS and other bodies with an interest in the health of the population. The fact that the health strategy drew inspiration, at ministers' insistence, from WHO's Health for All strategy only increased the interest in it.

What has Britain learned from the European experience?

It has to be stated at the outset that Britain was far more inclined to proselytise the virtues of the NHS reforms than to learn anything, or be receptive to advice, from European countries. After all, this was at a time when the Conservative Government under Mrs Thatcher's leadership was riding high in the world. Other leaders viewed her with a mix of incredulity and hostility. But love her or hate her, you could not ignore her. Consequently, the traffic flow was rather all one way, with ministers only too ready to sell the NHS reforms and to package them in such a way that any inconvenient flaws or blemishes were conveniently air-brushed out of the picture. Visitors to Britain always contrasted the view of the NHS reforms they got from central government with the very different views put before them when they visited academic centres or even ventured forth into the field to see the changes for themselves at first hand. Only the US experience humbled British government representatives at the time since, if anywhere was looked to for inspiration, it had to be the USA where the ideas of Alain Enthoven were especially timely and influential. His fingerprints could certainly be seen on the 1989 White Paper, *Working for Patients*. Much of the market rhetoric with its language of competition, contracts, incentives, devolved budgets and being responsive to user preferences came directly from the USA, which itself was in the process of reinventing government. Paradoxically, it was also in the throes of attempting (unsuccessfully, as it transpired) to reform its own chaotic and highly inefficient health care 'system'.

None of this should come as a surprise. Historically, Britain has been far less close to, or comfortable with, the European welfare tradition with its strong emphasis on, and commitment to, the solidarity principle. In this, as in so much else, Britain shunned the European experience in favour of its long-standing special relationship with the USA. Certainly, Mrs Thatcher valued this relationship to a far greater extent than anything closer to home. Indeed, as has been well documented, the whole European project was one she and fellow Conservatives were deeply sceptical of. Therefore, in health care as in other areas, there was reckoned to be little of value happening in Europe which might usefully inform policy-thinking in the UK. An instinctive xenophobia, mixed with deep hostility towards Europe, did not create an environment receptive to European thinking or experience – at least not officially or overtly. A good example of the British Conservative Government's negative response to most, if not all, things European was its refusal to sign the Ljubljana Charter on Reforming Health Care (although the Labour Government is likely to reverse this decision and sign the Charter). The Charter was prepared by WHO (Regional Office for Europe) at a conference of all member states in June 1996.[13] The Charter set out six fundamental principles governing health care reform in Europe (see Box 2) and a number of principles for managing change (see Box 3). The last of these – learning from experience – stressed the need to promote the national and international exchange of experience with implementing health care reform and supporting reform initiatives. The Charter insisted that any support must be founded on a well-validated knowledge base with regard to health care reforms, with cross-cultural differences in health care being properly understood and appropriately valued.

The general myopia prevailing in the British Government during the 1980s and early 1990s did not stop various commentators from urging the NHS to look to Europe for new thinking on, for example, the rationing dilemma, on long-term care in the community as well as residential care and nursing home provision. Although it was not appreciated at the time by our political leaders, during the early and mid-1990s Europe did hold up a mirror to the UK in respect of evidence documenting growing social and health inequalities which were significantly wider between social groups in the UK than

---

Box 2 Fundamental principles

European health care systems need to be:

Driven by values

Targeted on health

Centred on people

Focused on quality

Based on sound financing

Oriented towards primary health care

Source: World Health Organization[13]

Box 3 Principles for managing change

The following principles are key to managing change effectively:

Develop health policy

Listen to the citizen's voice and choice

Reshape health care delivery

Reorient human resources for health care

Strengthen management

Learn from experience

Source: World Health Organization[13]

---

elsewhere in Europe. Comparisons also continued to be made with Europe over the level of funding for health care, with Britain being seen to lag significantly behind average European levels of funding. But, as many observers have argued, Maxwell among them, it is not only a matter of capping budgets. 'The challenge is not merely to limit, but also to choose in an informed way where to set the limits, and to obtain the best results one can within those limits.'[14] (p.105) Adopting this view, Maxwell counselled that the management challenge not be confined to cost containment because it is in fact much more exciting. Regrettably, his advice has largely been ignored both in the UK and elsewhere.

With the election of the Labour Government in May 1997 bringing in its wake a more open and welcoming stance towards Europe, it seems likely that closer links at a trans-governmental level can be expected in matters concerning health policy and health care reform. Certainly, the European Commission is quietly preparing itself for a more explicit presence in the health care field. Hitherto it has been confined to aspects of public health but as the UK Government and others become more determined to tackle social exclusion and create sustainable healthy communities then the role of health services in contributing to progress in these areas also becomes more critical.

Moreover, no single European country can tackle the health, as distinct from health care, agenda in isolation. The challenge is by definition a trans-national one in which a degree of collective action is required.

Conclusion

Invariably, trans-national studies or commentaries end with a plea for improved lesson-learning or information-exchange mechanism. But however valuable and rewarding such a sharing of knowledge and hard-won experience may be, it remains questionable whether it in fact makes any difference to the course upon which a government has embarked or on which it is intent upon embarking. Nevertheless, the attempt to share knowledge and learn lessons is worth making in the hope that something rubs off and proves useful.

Robert Maxwell has always been of the persuasion that the potential for lesson-learning is not as fully exploited as it might be and that it can be of tremendous value even if at times it can also be a frustrating experience. If there are enduring lessons to be learned from the UK experience of health care reform stretching back over more than a quarter of a century then perhaps one would be hard pressed to improve on Maxwell's short list of three key lessons.[10] First, he advises, be as specific as possible about the problem(s) to be solved and avoid reaching too quickly for solutions. Second, resist the temptation continually to rejig the structure of health care delivery systems. And, finally, adopt an evolutionary approach to change showing a greater respect for evidence. For all their good intentions to follow this advice, governments find it unbelievably difficult to do so in practice. Maybe paying more attention to what other countries are doing would encourage a sharper awareness of what is happening in any single country. Certainly, the UK health care reform experience contains important lessons for other European countries and, in turn, their experiences could prove useful for us. Promoting the benefits of cross-national dialogue must continue.

References

1. OECD. Health care reform: the will to change. *Health Policy Studies* 1996; No. 8.
2. Bengoa R, Hunter DJ (eds). *New directions in managing health care*. Leeds: World Health Organization and Nuffield Institute for Health Services Studies, 1991.
3. WHO. *European health care reforms: analysis of current strategies*. Copenhagen: WHO, 1996.
4. OECD. Internal markets in the making. *Health Policy Studies* 1995; No. 6.
5. Ham C, Hunter DJ, Robinson R. Evidence based policy-making. *British Medical Journal* 1995; 310:71.
6. Klein R. *The new politics of the NHS*. 3rd edn. London: Longman, 1995.
7. Coote A, Hunter DJ. *New agenda for health*. London: Institute for Public Policy Research, 1996.
8. Robinson R, Le Grand J (eds). *Evaluating the NHS reforms*. London: King's Fund Institute, 1994.
9. Figueras J, Saltman R, Mossialos E. *Challenges in evaluating health sector reform: an overview*. LSE Health Discussion Paper No. 8. London: The London School of Economics and Political Science, 1997.
10. Maxwell RJ. The limits of simple fixes. In: Glouberman S (ed). *Beyond restructuring*. London: King's Fund, 1996.
11. Schön D. *Beyond the stable state*. Harmondsworth: Penguin, 1974.
12. Ham C (ed). *Health care reform: learning from international experience*. Buckingham: Open University Press, 1997.
13. WHO. *European health care reforms: The Ljubljana Charter on Reforming Health Care*. Copenhagen: WHO, 1996.
14. Maxwell RJ. *Health and wealth: an international study of health-care spending*. Massachusetts: Lexington Books, 1981.

Health economics
in Britain:
an incomplete
history

Alan Maynard
Professor of Health Economics
York Health Economics Consortium, University of York

Over a little more than a quarter of a century the subdiscipline of health economics in Britain has grown from practically nothing to a major industry with increasing influence on policy-making. The purposes of this essay are to offer an incomplete and personal review of the history of that growth and to discuss whether the economic approach is merely 'a bastard science and an insidious poison in the body politic', or an essential ingredient into policy-making.

What is health economics?

Economics is usually described as the science of how choices are made when resources are scarce and there are many competing purposes for which they can be used. In health care, the ubiquitous existence of scarcity means that decision-makers – be they doctors, managers, civil servants or politicians – have to make harsh choices about what services to provide, how to provide them, how much to provide, and to whom to provide them. All choices have an opportunity cost: a decision to create GP fundholding left fewer resources to direct at the improvement in quality of 'poor' GP practices in deprived city centres. A decision to treat Peter Jones with a coronary artery bypass graft deprives John Smith of a hip replacement. Thus Jones' life may be saved, but Smith is left in pain and discomfort.

The health economist's toolkit is often thought to be narrow and largely concerned with the economic evaluation of therapeutic interventions in particular. This is a mistake. The range of issues which can be explored with the use of economics is much broader, as is illustrated in Figure 1.

The first thing a health economist emphasises is that he or she is a specialist in the analysis not just of health care, but of health. Health is influenced by many factors, such as genetic endowments, income, wealth, education, housing, work environment and leisure pursuits. The study of the relative effects of these factors and health care in improving the length and quality of patients' lives is of importance, but poorly developed, in part, because of the absence of appropriate data sets.[1]

Any evaluation of health care and other inputs into the health production process requires a measure of success, i.e. health. The history of health status or outcome measurement is long and the available measures remain contentious but useful.[2,3] Such measures

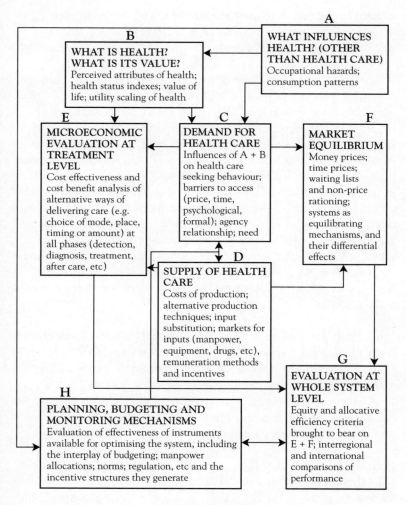

Figure 1 Health economics – has it fulfilled its potential?

are also an essential ingredient into the 'industry' of 'health care evaluation' (Figure 1, box E). This is the area of health economics in which most resources have been invested and where the majority of health economists have made a living. It remains contentious because of the drive for consensus about methods (the guidelines industry) which tends to mask the lack of agreement about appropriate approaches in significant areas of evaluative practice (these issues will be discussed further below).

While most resources have gone into economic evaluation, the potential productivity of many of the other areas of applied economics in health and health care is large and has been neglected. The determinants of patient demand for health care, both monetary and non-monetary (e.g. time travel costs) are areas in which there has been little research. To the extent that prices influence patient demand, that is by the use of co-payments, there is nice controversy. The US Rand Corporation experiment demonstrated that while user charges reduced patient utilisation of health care, the effects on patient health status of reduced used might not be great.[4] These results are contentious. For instance, a group of Canadians concluded that 'user charges are misguided and cynical attempts to tax the ill and/or drive up the total cost of health care while shifting some of the burden out of government budgets'.[5]

Inherent in the arguments about the costs and benefits of user charges is an ideological dispute, as well as disagreements about evidence. Many US health economists are more prepared to accept willingness and ability to pay as the determinant of access to health care. In Canada and western Europe, the consensus favours access determined largely by need, where 'need' is defined as the patient's ability to benefit from care per unit cost.

Both groups accept that both private insurance and state alternatives (like the UK NHS) abolish the price barrier to consumption and, in so doing, create moral hazard, i.e. a propensity to consume health care when the benefits at the margin are less than the marginal cost. Such behaviour is made possible because third party pays, i.e. the insurer or Government, rather than the user, finances health care.

While some of these issues (Figure 1, box C) have been explored well, some of the subjects associated with the supply of health have been ignored. For instance, research into the labour market has neglected the issue of skill mix until quite recently.[6] As a consequence, important questions, such as whether and to what extent nurses and pharmacists can be substituted for general practitioners, remain areas of policy dispute with Government discounting their importance and planning to expand medical school intake considerably.

Another important supply-side issue is the remuneration of doctors and hospitals. Which methods of doctor payment, for instance, induce cost containment, efficiency and equity? The reform of the GP contract in 1990 introduced fees which induced GPs to produce much higher levels of vaccination, immunisation and cervical cytology. However, this success has not been matched by innovation in hospital doctor payment systems where 'distinction awards' may be of dubious efficiency.[7]

With demand exceeding the supply of health care, rationing is unavoidable. However, this word is very emotive and brings with it denials from politicians, in particular, that it either exists or should be explicit. Yet, rationing is ubiquitous, and in the NHS waiting time, money prices (e.g. for drugs) and clinical decisions determine who gets what treatment, if any, and when. The current system is to let local NHS purchasers decide, and this results in gross inequalities with patients on one side of the street being given particular types of care and those on the other side being denied it. Such inequalities are created by politicians' refusal to define explicit rationing criteria.[8,9,10]

Most health care reforms, better known as 'redisorganisations', tend to be implemented rapidly, often with little or no reference to the knowledge base, and evaluated reluctantly. Thus the UK internal market reforms were developed rapidly with little reference to evidence and implemented swiftly, with the Government arguing that evaluation was not only irrelevant, but it would delay change. As a consequence, much of the 1989–91 NHS reforms are regarded as a success by some politicians but their rhetoric cannot be sustained by evidence.[11]

Box H in Figure 1 contains subjects about the effectiveness of macro- and micro-mechanisms in optimising the health care system as a whole. All health care structures contain incentives, some explicit, some implicit, some consistent with the pursuit of system goals, and some so perverse that they frustrate the achievement of policy objectives. Not only is it necessary to define and evaluate this interaction, but also to accept that regulation is unavoidable.

Those who advocate 'free markets' are lost in an ideological dream: no markets are free! Coase, a US Nobel Laureate and pro-market economist, when discussing the working of stock and futures markets, noted that:

> It is not without significance that these exchanges, often used by economists as examples of a perfect market and perfect competition, are markets in which transactions are highly regulated (and this quite apart from any government regulation that there may be). It suggests, I think correctly, that for anything approaching perfect competition to exist, an intricate system of rules and regulations would normally be needed.[12]

Thus, as is evident from Figure 1, the scope for the deployment of economic techniques of analysis is considerable but, over the first 25 years of its existence, the subdiscipline of health economics has developed very unevenly.

Some achievements in health economics

During the first quarter of a century of its development, health economics has had some significant impacts, both on intellectual development and policy. Some examples of this are budget allocation, outcome measurement and economic evaluation.

Budget allocation formulae

Culyer and Cooper wrote extensively about the inequalities in budget allocation describing separately and independently the distributional inequities analysed previously by Feldstein.[13,14,15] By the late 1960s, this work had impacted on the Government, with the then Minister,

Richard Crossman, declaring it was the most significant policy problem he confronted.

However, it was left to his Conservative successor, Keith Joseph, to implement a budget allocation formula designed to mitigate the inequalities in per capita financial capacity in the 14 English NHS regions. Following criticism of this, the Resource Allocation Working Party (RAWP) proposed a new formula for hospital and community health services which was published in 1976, and used until 1990.[16] In the early 1990s, there were two revisions of the RAWP formula. Subsequently, a group at York University was commissioned to renew the formula, and their proposals have now been fully implemented.[17]

Thus work started by economists was translated into an innovative formula (RAWP) in collaboration with epidemiologists (e.g. Walter Holland), with separate models in Wales, Scotland and Ulster. These formulae equalised financial capacity considerably within each constituent part of the UK, but not between them.[18,19] The new York formula will equalise financed capacity further, moving it from the relatively well-endowed rural areas of Wessex and Oxford to the deprived urban areas of London and the North. However, as yet, no budget allocation for primary care has been implemented.[20]

Outcome measurement

When Alan Williams was seconded by the Treasury to the Ministry of Health in the late 1960s, his critique of the current hospital building plan included advocacy of investment related to health improvement. This required a measure of health outcome – a challenge which drove Williams' career for nearly 30 years.[21,22]

This work was developed initially with York colleagues, Culyer and Lavers, then with a psychiatrist, Rachel Rosser, and subsequently with the York Euro-Qol Group. This progression took Williams from health indicators, to the use of Rosser's innovative work using disability and distress descriptors of health, to the production of quality-adjusted life year (QALY) estimates of the value of competing therapies, and then to the dissemination of the Euro-Qol.[3] Obviously, Williams was not the only researcher, let alone economist, involved in this work but much of the literature is influenced, if not dominated, by his work.

Economic evaluation

Again, the influence of Williams, an academic with interests in public finance before his 'baptism' in the Ministry of Health in the late 1960s, is of central importance. By the mid-1970s, he had published a checklist or guideline for the practice of economic evaluation which is the original of the myriad of checklists and guidelines which have appeared subsequently (see Figure 2).[23]

A basic checklist of questions runs as follows:
1. What precisely is the question which the study was trying to answer?
2. What is the question that it has actually answered?
3. What are the assumed objectives of the activity studied?
4. By what measures are these represented?
5. How are they weighted?
6. Do they enable us to tell whether the objectives are being attained?
7. What range of options was considered?
8. What other options might there have been?
9. Were they rejected, or not considered, for good reasons?
10. Would their inclusion have been likely to change the results?
11. Is anyone likely to be affected who has not been considered in the analysis?
12. If so, why are they excluded?
13. Does the notion of cost go wider or deeper than the expenditure of the agency concerned?
14. If not, is it clear that these expenditures cover all the resources used and accurately represent their value if released for other uses?
15. If so, is the line drawn so as to include all potential beneficiaries and losers, and are resources costed at their value in their best alternative use?
16. Is the differential timing of the items in the streams of benefits and costs suitably taken care of (e.g. by discounting, and, if so, at what rate)?
17. Where there is uncertainty or known margins of error, is it made clear how sensitive the outcome is to these elements?
18. Are the results, on balance, good enough for the job in hand?
19. Has anyone else done better?

Source: Williams[23]

Figure 2 The Williams guidelines for economic evaluation

Williams' graduate supervision of Michael Drummond led to the production of a text by the latter on the economic evaluation of health care and the first collection of systematically appraised case studies in this area.[24,25] Drummond has subsequently skilfully synthesised and developed the techniques of economic evaluation.[26,27]

However, while the 'art form' has developed, there remain contentious issues. First, there is the risk that the drive for guidelines and checklists will mask areas of dispute and produce a phoney consensus which will lead to poor studies, which will in turn corrupt the knowledge base.[28,29,30]

Second, economists, like their clinical colleagues, have demonstrated that while they may be *taught* 'good practice' in economic evaluation, they do not *practise* it. This may be due to lack of skill or the problem of commercial influences 'diverting' practitioners into design, execution and reporting of studies which is less than complete. Such outcomes may, in part, be the product of incomplete knowledge. Thus, in the early stages of the development of a new drug, efficacy data may be based on small trials with short follow-ups of patients. Modelling with such data is a difficult exercise requiring explicitness about assumptions and careful sensitivity analysis.

The third problem with economic evaluation in health care is that all is not agreed as to how it should be practised. For example, which health outcome measures should be used? What is the empirical basis of the discount rate used in these studies? Why are economists rarely concerned with sample size, while clinicians and statisticians are fixated with this issue?

Argument and opinion about these and other issues are nicely set out in recent books.[31,27] They are of great policy importance because it seems likely that other countries will follow the example of Australia, where, since 1991, reimbursement decisions on drugs have been informed by the results of economic evaluation.[32] If the reimbursement (and hence the use) of drugs in the NHS is to be influenced by economic evaluation, it is essential that there is commercial neutrality and careful audit of the work of practitioners.

Some emerging areas

While health economists have made some significant developments in both the methods and application of their techniques of analysis in the last 25 years, investments in some areas have been parsimonious.

For instance, the application of the techniques of industrial economics to the pharmaceutical industry and to the health care industry have been modest. The drug industry is a ubiquitous policy problem, being accused of 'high' prices and cost inflation. Analysis of the industry is limited[33] or dated[34] and evaluation of it in terms of structure, conduct and performance is slight. One obstacle to more analytical work is the difficulty of accessing data, but much more could be done to develop the knowledge base about how to regulate better this industry which is, due to patent legislation and profit regulation, a creature of the State (or perhaps the State is creature of the industry?!).

With the creation of the NHS internal market, the relevance of industrial economics to the analysis and evaluation of hospital trusts and other market services, such as contracting, became very evident. However, initial funding of such research was meagre, and it was only towards the end of the Major Administration that work in this area developed inside and outside the Government.[35]

Systematic appraisal of some of this industry research has produced some pertinent policy information which the new Labour Government seems intent on ignoring. The NHS Centre for Reviews and Dissemination concluded that evidence of economies of scale in hospitals beyond 600 beds was limited.[36] Yet the Government is adopting ambitious merger policies.

A final area of industrial economics which has begun to develop is anti-trust regulation. However, this work has been developed outside academia with the Monopolies Commission criticising fee cartels in the private insurance industry[37] and the Office of Fair Trading advocating both better regulation or private insurers and the abolition of resale price maintenance on over-the-counter drugs.[38,39]

In labour economics, the amount of research in the health economics area remains small with the growth, if anywhere, most evident in government, in particular association with the Pay Review bodies (which determine the pay of doctors, dentists, nurses and professions allied to medicine) and the Standing Commission on the Physician Workforce. It is notable how the issues dealt with by these bodies have been researched by consultancy groups rather than by University academics. The continuing reluctance of many academic economists to apply their skill to these issues is remarkable.

An area in which academic economists have taken a lead, even when the political climate was thoroughly unacceptable, has been in equity. The European Union financed a path-breaking study which involved the application of a common research methodology to ten countries. This demonstrated, *inter alia*, that high health care spenders had less inequality in morbidity, with the exception of the USA.[40] Subsequent work by the group has sought to appraise the effects of recent health care reform on inequality. They found that the impact of reform in nine countries was limited and that inequalities in self-assessed health were particularly marked in the UK and the USA.[41,42]

The future of health economics

If governments create a 'fourth hurdle' of regulation for the pharmaceutical industry, considerable employment will be generated for economists! At present, industry has to demonstrate safety, efficacy and quality (three hurdles) before it can acquire a product licence and sell its drug. The creation of an economic (fourth) hurdle to ensure that reimbursement or rationing decisions are based on cost and effectiveness data seems likely as governments seek to control drug expenditure and target it to maximise improvements in health status.

Despite such investments, it is likely that health economics, as a subdiscipline, will broaden both in terms of the application and development of basic theory and the increased use of quantitative methods. A major difference between health economics in the UK

and in the USA is that US researchers have access to much better data sets. In the USA, private as well as public agencies carry out regular surveys of hospital utilisation, consumer behaviour and expenditure. These provide a rich source of material which can be used to test hypotheses and explore the behaviour of producers and consumers. The Rand insurance experiment cost over $75 million to design, implement and report, and even more modest investments than this can create significant new knowledge.

However, British policy-makers do not wish to be confused by facts. The NHS is remarkable in that it operates often largely in the absence of data about fundamental aspects of its operations. As a consequence, questions such as 'why do patients go to see GPs?' can be answered only poorly. What is needed is investment in better data so that the NHS market, whatever form it takes under the new Government, can be analysed more carefully and lessons drawn to inform future reforms. Some of this investment in data should be on longitudinal studies. At present the majority of longitudinal surveys include limited economics data, and this makes difficult, among other things, appraisals of the relative importance of the many factors which influence health.[1]

While the economists have 'colonised' clinical minds during the last 25 years and convinced them of the merits of measuring the costs and effects (in terms of enhanced health status) of competing interventions, they have failed to convince research funders and policy-makers that there is more to health economics than economic evaluation. The potential contribution from developing R&D funding to cover labour, capital and industrial aspects of the NHS is large. It would, for instance, illuminate the issues of how best to regulate the pharmaceutical industry and how to supervise better the performance and behaviour of private insurers and private providers.

Slowly, the discipline of health economics is developing and contributing more fully to the processes of policy formulation. In the next 25 years it will continue to grow, although its precise development path, apart from being more theoretical and more quantitative, is difficult to foresee and will, inevitably, be affected by the foresight and preferences of the next generation of leading health economists.

References

1. Grossman M. *The demand for health: a theoretical and empirical investigation.* New York: National Bureau for Economics Research, 1974.
2. Stewart AL, Ware JE (eds). *Measuring functioning and well-being.* Durham and London: Durham University Press, 1992.
3. EuroQol Group. EuroQol: a new facility for the measurement of health related quality of life. *Health Policy* 1990; 16:199–208
4. Newhouse JP, Manning WG, Morris CM. *Some internal results from a controlled final of cost sharing in health insurance.* 1981.
5. Stoddart G, Barer M, Evans R. *User charges, snares and delusions, another look at the literature.* Ontario: Premiers' Council on Health, Well Being and Social Justice, 1994.
6. Jenkins-Clarke S, Carr-Hill R. *Skill-mix in primary care: executive summary.* York: Centre for Health Economics, University of York, 1997.
7. Bloor K, Maynard A. *Rewarding excellence? Consultants distinction award and the need for reform.* Discussion Paper. York: Centre for Health Economics, University of York, 1992.
8. New B. *The rationing agenda in the NHS.* London: King's Fund, 1996.
9. Maynard A. Rationing health care. *British Medical Journal* 1996; 313:1499.
10. Maynard A. Evidence based medicine: on incomplete methods for informing treatment choices. *Lancet* 1997; 349:126–8
11. Maynard A, Bloor K. Introducing a market to the United Kingdom's National Health Service. *New England Journal of Medicine* 1996; 334:604–8.
12. Coase R. *The firm, the market and the law.* Chicago: University of Chicago Press, 1988.
13. Cooper MH, Culyer AJ. *An economic assessment of some aspects of the operation of the NHS.* Health Services Financing, a report of the British Medical Association, 1970.
14. Cooper MH, Culyer AJ. Equality in the NHS: intentions, performance and problems in evaluation. In: Howser MM (ed). *The economics of medical care.* London: Allen and Unwin, 1972.
15. Feldstein, MS. Economic analysis for health services efficiency. Amsterdam: North Holland, 1967.
16. Department of Health and Social Security. *Sharing resources for health in England: report of the Resource Allocation Working Party.* London: HMSO, 1976.

17. Peacock S, Smith P. *The resource allocation consequences of the new NHS needs formula*. Discussion Paper 134. York: Centre for Health Economics, University of York, 1995.

18. Maynard A, Ludbrook A. Applying resource allocation to the constituent parts of the United Kingdom. *Lancet* 1980; 85–87:8158.

19. Birch S, Maynard A. *The RAWP review: RAWPing primary care and RAWPing the UK*. Discussion Paper. York: Centre for Health Economics, University of York, 1986.

20. Bloor K, Maynard A. *Equity in primary care*. Discussion Paper 141. York: Centre for Health Economics, University of York, 1995.

21. Culyer AJ, Maynard A (eds). *Being reasonable about health economics*. London: Edward Elgar, 1997.

22. Maynard A, Sheldon T. Health economics: has it fulfilled its promise? In: Maynard A, Chalmers I (eds). *Non-random reflections in health services research: on the 25th Anniversary of Archie Cochrane's effectiveness and efficiency*. 1997.

23. Williams A. The cost-benefit approach. *British Medical Bulletin* 1974; 30(3):252–6

24. Drummond MF. *Principles of economic analysis, health care*. Oxford: Oxford University Press, 1980.

25. Drummond MF. *Studies in economic appraisal in health care*. Oxford: Oxford University Press, 1981.

26. Drummond MF, Stoddart G, Torrance G. *Methods of economic evaluation in health care programmes*. Oxford: Oxford University Press, 1987.

27. Drummond MF, O'Brien B, Stoddart G, Torrance G. *Methods for economic evaluation in health care programmes*. 2nd edn. Oxford: Oxford University Press, 1997.

28. Evans RE. Manufacturing consensus, marketing truth: guidelines for economic evaluation. *Annual of Internal Medicine* 1995; 123(1):59–60.

29. Maynard A. Economic evaluation techniques in health care: re-inventing the wheel. *Pharmacoeconomics* 1997; 11(2):115–18.

30. Reinhardt U. Making economic evaluation respectable. *Social Science and Medicine* 1997; 45(4):455–62.

31. Gold MR, Siegal JE, Russell LB, Weistein MC. *Cost effectiveness in health and medicine*. New York: Oxford University Press, 1996.

32. Maynard A, Bloor K. Regulating the pharmaceutical industry. *British Medical Journal* 1997; 315:200–1.

33. Reekie WD. *Economics of the pharmaceutical industry*. London: Macmillan, 1975.

34. Cooper MH. *Prices and profits in the pharmaceutical industry*. Oxford: Pergamon, 1966.

35. Goddard M, Ferguson B. *Mergers in the NHS: made in heaven or marriages of convenience?* Health Economics Occasional Paper 3. London: Nuffield Trust, 1997.

36. NHS Centre for Reviews and Dissemination. *Concentration and choice in the provision of hospital services*. CRD Report 8. York: University of York, 1997.
37. Monopolies and Mergers Commission. *Private medical services: report on agreements and practices relating to changes for the supply of private medical services by NHS consultants*. Cm 2452. London: HMSO, 1994.
38. Office of Fair Trading. *Health insurance: a report*. London: Office of Fair Trading, 1996.
39. Office of Fair Trading. *Over the counter medicine: a report*. London: Office of Fair Trading, 1996.
40. Van Doorslaer E, Wagstaff A, Rutten F. *Equity in the finance and delivery of health care: an international perspective*. Oxford: Oxford Medical Publications, 1993.
41. Van Doorslaer E, Wagstaff A, Bleichrodt G, Calonge UG *et al*. Income related inequalities in health: some international comparisons. *Journal of Health Economics* 1997; 16(1):93–112
42. Propper C. *Who pays for and who gets health care: equity in the finance and delivery of health care in the UK*. Health Economics Occasional Paper 5. London: Nuffield Trust, 1997.

A tale
out of school,
or reflections on
the management
of the National
Health Service

Nicholas Timmins
Public Policy Editor, Financial Times

Genuinely new ideas in social policy are incredibly rare. That, as much as anything, explains why the National Health Service found itself launching an internal market in 1991. The old health authorities became progressively divided from the hospitals they used to manage. The hospitals became self-governing institutions, free to sell their wares to any health authority that would buy in a purchaser/provider split. Each became freer to deal with the private sector. And GP fundholders were set up to provide an alternative purchaser, allowed to control significant parts of their own budgets and use them to acquire secondary and community care.

Why was the internal market adopted? Because it was the only new idea in town in 1988 – the year the Government found itself forced by the worst financial crisis in the Health Service's 40-year history to launch an NHS review which it had neither planned nor wanted.

Desperately casting around for a change to make once the review was up and running, the Government had available as a blueprint only the ideas of Alain Enthoven, the health management specialist from Stanford University. Back in 1984, he had been invited over by the Nuffield Provincial Hospitals Trust to take a 'sympathetic' look at the NHS. His recommendations, in the numbskullingly boringly titled *Reflections on the management of the National Health Service*,[1] contained a loose outline of the ideas which later became the internal market – and which in time came to affect (or infect, depending on your point of view) health care systems around the world, from the UK to The Netherlands and New Zealand.

Before the review settled on the internal market, however, it had started by examining a clutch of ideas for re-financing the NHS. These included introducing new charges, tax relief for all for private health cover, a switch to social insurance and a hypothecated tax from which individuals would then be allowed to opt out if they took private health insurance. In time, all these ideas were rejected.

When the review's outcome was published in February 1989, the only trace of those ideas that remained was the introduction of tax relief on private health insurance for people aged over 60 – a measure which did little to increase the private health care market, and which the incoming Labour Government promptly scrapped, seven years later, in the first budget after its election win in 1997.

The same Labour Government had also pledged itself to abolish the internal market – although precisely what that was to mean was far from clear. It was, however, clear that ten years on from the crisis which led to the NHS review, some things had moved full circle. Not in the sense, by any means, that there was to be a full return to life before 1991. The wheel had moved on, and some form of purchaser/provider split was to remain. But the market was now plainly to be much more managed and controlled than it had been even under the Conservatives – when a fair degree of management had remained for fear of what would happen to health service provision if a fully blooded competitive market in health care were allowed to operate unchecked.

'Full circle' is perhaps overstating it. But some elements of the way the NHS was to be run under the Blair Government would clearly bear more similarity to the way the NHS was starting to develop between 1984 and 1988, than they would to what could have happened had Conservative ministers been brave or foolish enough to allow market forces to operate unrestricted.

This thought, in a personal book that should contain at least some personal memories, perhaps makes it worth recalling and reflecting on an afternoon at the Department of Health on 13 July 1993. It was sultry and summery, and Sir Roy Griffiths's then still deputy chairman of the NHS supervisory board, was being interviewed by the author for the book which became *The Five Giants*.[2]

The NHS owes more to Roy Griffiths than it is probably able to acknowledge. When the full history of the service is written, it is no doubt the 1991 changes on which historians will focus. The wise ones, however, may well see that the more seminal event was almost certainly Sir Roy Griffiths's 'letter' to Norman Fowler, the then Secretary of State for Social Services, in 1983: the outcome of his inquiry into NHS management.

Easily the most unconventional NHS report of all time, Griffiths's 20 pages of diagnosis and recommendation called for the introduction of general management into the NHS – noting in his graphic phrase that 'if Florence Nightingale were carrying her lamp through the corridors of the NHS today, she would almost certainly be looking for the people in charge'.[3]

In many ways, this was the real turning point for the service. His call for consensus management to go, and for managers to replace administrators, both in the health services and in the Department of Health, was, at least arguably, the saving of the NHS. It started the process which brought doctors back into management. This role a few had held as medical superintendents of hospitals back in the 1940s and 1950s, and this had been developing slowly for other doctors through the 1960s via the Cogwheel system: a process destroyed by Sir Keith Joseph's 1974 reorganisation of the NHS. Roy's report provided health authorities, and in time hospitals, both with someone clearly responsible for the decisions which had to be taken, and with, for the first time, a recognisable line-management system. It is a change whose importance is difficult to overstate, for without it the 1991 NHS reforms would never have happened – for the very simple reason that there would have been no one there to deliver them.

Over a couple of hours and more that afternoon Roy went back over all this and the NHS review of which, as Margaret Thatcher's personal adviser on health care management, he was the only non-ministerial member. He was in good form, amusing, often pithy, quite pointed.

In his later years, with his drawn face and high-domed forehead, set slightly too large for absolute proportion above a body slimmed down by the weight he had lost after his coronary artery by-pass, Sir Roy Griffiths looked increasingly like a cross between Alec Guinness as ObiWan-Kenobi and the Martian-like latex puppet Yoda: the two wise and all-knowing Jedi knights from *Star Wars*. He could, when he chose, be as authoritative as Guinness and as elusive and allusive as Yoda – something John Moore was to discover when Roy, ahead of the publication of his second report on community care, went in to explain that he planned to hand control of it over to local authorities: a message that Norman Fowler's ill-fated successor appears not to have heard, despite Roy being clear that he delivered it.

Although deeply committed to the health service, Griffiths had not been seen as such when he was first appointed to run the management inquiry in 1983. The managing director of Sainsbury's during one of its most successful and expansionary periods, he was instantly labelled as an archetypal Thatcherite businessman. His appointment came only six months after the leak of a report from the Central Policy Review Staff, the Cabinet Office think-tank, which had suggested replacing the NHS with privatised health insurance as a way of meeting some extremely gloomy forecasts about the likely future cost of the welfare state. The report had been instantly shelved. But suspicions remained that the long-term goal of the Tories was still to privatise the NHS. There were bitter jibes, which now sound almost antediluvian, asking what on earth supermarkets had to do with health care? What could a grocer like Griffiths possibly know, contribute or care?

Griffiths, however, did care, although quite how much he may at times have concealed from Margaret Thatcher, the Prime Minister. The son of a colliery overman in North Staffordshire, he had been a Bevin boy, sent down the mines at the end of the Second World War before an Oxford scholarship, a brief spell with the National Coal Board and then a career first with Monsanto and then with Sainsbury's. He also had childhood memories of the 1930s depression, of 'five bob to go and see the doctor' and of what he described as 'the great and glorious days' of the Beveridge report.

When his report came out, he faced an angry meeting of 300 nurses in the Bloomsbury Hotel who booed and hissed him, an experience which physically took him aback, leaving him stunned and hurt. His report would mean that nurses would eventually lose the elaborate administrative hierarchy they had built up in the wake of the Salmon report, but they would in return get the chance to manage. The nurses' response was to run one of the wittier campaigns of protest which the NHS has seen, with adverts arguing that the NHS in future would be run by people 'who don't know their coccyx from their humerus'.

On that afternoon in July 1993, Roy went back over all this, telling stories of the review, of Mrs Thatcher's attitude to the NHS – 'She would have liked to have got away from it: if it hadn't been there, she would never have invented it' – while analysing acutely the heady days he'd lived through. Towards the end, he suddenly asked to go off the record.

At this point, the NHS market was more than two years old. It was more than four years since the White Paper outlining it had been published by Kenneth Clarke, Secretary of State for Health, with the most extravagant launch any White Paper has ever enjoyed.

'This,' Roy said, 'is absolutely not for the record. But Clarke said to me on one occasion, "I wish to God we had never got into this review, because we could have taken things on just as a natural, quiet extension of your management proposals. If we had worked on it on that basis, we wouldn't have had all this hullabaloo." His feeling wasn't for the market. His feeling was for an orderly managed process, as it were.'

But surely, as time went by, Clarke, who fought a bitter, rough-housing battle with the British Medical Association and the Labour Party over the reforms, had become converted to them in his period as health secretary?

'I don't think so,' Roy said. 'Not very converted. He became converted to it, but not very. I think that comment to me was very significant. You see, when you talk about the market, what are you talking about? You are simply saying that someone with money can place it either here or there. Now, you can do that in a direct managed situation, or you can do it through contracts. And I don't think Ken saw the market being the main driving force at all: which it isn't. You can see what's happened. Very few people have moved contracts about. If they did so to any great extent there would be a fine bloody uproar.

'The difference between the health service and the private sector is that in the private sector there is generally somewhere else to go. If Sainsbury's drop a contract with somebody, that somebody can always go to Asda, Tesco, Marks and Spencer or whoever. In the health service, it is nice to think you can go to another district health authority if you lose a contract, but you can't really. So by and large, they don't get moved much.'

The whole review, he said, was ' far too sophisticated for the state of the health service as it was in 1987,' and in terms of the outcome from it, 'I still remain to be persuaded about these things'.

Roy had, he said, favoured an experiment with health maintenance-type organisations where the GPs would be given money to buy specialist care. 'I believed in that because I believed the health service is big enough for experiment. But I felt at the time that it was an absolute prerequisite, before we got into anything sophisticated, to get the running of the hospitals and the information base much more satisfactory. Then would have been the time to go ahead with GP fundholding.

'It was a tremendous step to move away from the line management to the contractual approach. You can point out the similarities. In both cases you are concentrating on outcomes. In line management, when you start up a budgetary process the essence of it is very simply that you spell out what you are wanting for the input of certain money. But you then retain your line-management role. So if things are going wrong, you can intervene, you can change the managers, put things right.

'In a contractual situation, you are saying "we aren't concerned with the means. We are simply concerned with the outcomes, and we will pay for that". To go off the line-management responsibility, without any feel for outcomes at all – still – for even at this point they are very embryonic, is I thought then and still think now, far too sophisticated.'

GP fundholding, he said, had indeed brought its gains. 'It changes the basis of power in the health service. It will make the consultants take much more notice of the GPs and so on, and that is absolutely central as far as I am concerned.

'But we set it up on the basis that the first GP fundholders were very lavishly endowed. You would have been mad not to go for GP fundholding from an economic point of view. Secondly you can reap the wild advantages of GP fundholding in the sense that you can do deals with the hospitals to get your patients into hospital early simply because you have GPs paying on a case basis, set against block contracts. A hospital with a block contract knows that anything that comes from a GP fundholder is sheer bunce. So you go for that. The block contract is so imprecise.

'But as it develops, two to three years out, the attitude of the district health authorities will be different. They will be saying to the hospitals, "If you start doing fancy deals with GP fundholders, then you don't get our business. That's what you would do in the commercial world". We have a ludicrous situation at the moment where the small man is running rings round the chap who holds all the contracts and all the power. I think it is too complicated and too sophisticated for the health service at the moment. And I have felt that since it began.'

Which, if it had been on the record, would at the time have been the stuff of a front-page story – 'Prime Minister's adviser opposes NHS reforms', or something similar. But this wasn't for a piece of journalism, it was for a book, and it was off the record. But Roy wanted it said. Which is why, four further years on and as a tale out of school, so to speak, it seems right to break the embargo.*

It is worth asking why he wanted it said. Roy may have believed in the NHS, but he was no sepia-tinted nostalgic about it. He was a powerful businessman. His management report had done more to change the NHS and help it stand a chance of surviving for the 21st century than any other report in its history, save perhaps for Guillebaud's in 1956, which demonstrated that the cost of the NHS was not outstripping the nation's ability to pay.

The management inquiry was certainly more important than the 1979 Royal Commission on the NHS of which Roy was contemptuously dismissive – 'It got half a day's debate in Parliament and was then put back in the wastepaper basket,' he said. Equally, he was not

---

*In Roy's absence, his widow, Lady Griffiths, has given permission for the quotes to be used.

against markets, or at least markets in the right place. Indeed, he had argued for them. One of the many other sources for the idea of a purchaser/provider split was Roy himself. In February 1988, just a fortnight after the NHS review was launched, Griffiths had delivered his other big report to Government: the one on community care. That argued that while local authorities should take the lead in organising the service, they should by no means attempt to provide it all. They should buy it in from whoever offered the best value, deliberately stimulating the private and voluntary sectors to provide a 'mixed economy' of care. 'This is a key statement,' the report said. 'The role of the public sector is essentially to ensure that care is provided. How it is provided is an important but secondary consideration and local authorities must show that they are getting and providing real value.'[4]

This was not an original idea: indeed it chimed with *The local right*,[5] a pamphlet published around the same time by Nicholas Ridley, the Environment Secretary and a Thatcherite, who was perhaps a truer believer in the doctrine even than Mrs Thatcher herself. That had argued for local authorities becoming 'enablers not providers', running everything on contract, although it had not descended to the detail of working out how that could apply to social services. Roy had. He was, therefore, clearly not against these ideas for the Health Service in principle. His reservations, rather, were practical.

There could be another explanation: that by 1993, Roy was less in the loop than he had been. From being the star of the first Griffiths report who was actually offered the job of being the first chief executive of the NHS ahead of Victor Paige (Mrs Thatcher badly wanted him to do it, but John Sainsbury felt he could not be spared from the supermarket group), Roy by 1993 was less central to the NHS's future than he had been between 1983 and 1991. By the time of the interview he was retired from Sainsbury's. There is a suspicion that he felt that he was listened to less than he should have been, and that the contribution he had made was less recognised than it might have been. Like the rest of us, he valued being valued. There might have been a touch of sour grapes.

But that won't really do: not least because the criticisms of the market that Roy was voicing in 1993 still in large measure hold four years further down the road. Contracts are still relatively rarely moved. Outcome measures, while improving, remain crude. Purchasers, in the main, are still low down on the learning curve. Anyone who shifts a big contract still risks destabilising the hospital affected so that prices for other procedures simply rise. There isn't a proper market in the NHS and the whole exercise has proved, as Roy put it, rather too sophisticated – certainly in terms of the measurable benefits it has brought.

And slowly, now, it looks as though a Labour government is set to move away from it: or at least away from the model as it was originally conceived. The purchaser/provider divide will remain. Something called contracts, or perhaps health care or service agreements, will continue. But they are likely to be closer to the model that Griffiths was talking about in 1993 than to the case-by-case purchasing based on detailed costings of individual treatments which some argued in the mid-1990s was the way that the NHS should move. It is worth noting that the other countries who adopted what might be dubbed the 'Enthoven model' – New Zealand certainly and The Netherlands to a lesser degree – have also moved rapidly away from the purer forms of contractual markets to something much more managed: a way of providing health services which is contestable, certainly, but much less commercially competitive than the theory suggested it should be. Had Roy still been here to see it, he would probably have smiled that slow smile of his and said, 'I told you so'.

References

1. Enthoven A. *Reflections on the management of the National Health Service*. Nuffield Provincial Hospitals Trust, Occasional Paper 5, 1985.
2. Timmins N. *The five giants: a biography of the welfare state*. Fontana Press, 1996 and HarperCollins, 1995.
3. Griffiths R. *NHS Management Inquiry* (The Griffiths Report). DHSS, 1983. For an account of the creation of the inquiry see *The Five Giants*, op. cit., pp 408–10.
4. Griffiths R. *Community Care: An agenda for action*. London: HMSO, 1988.

A democratic NHS: oxymoron or achievable goal?

Rudolf Klein
Professor of Social Policy, University of Bath,
and Professorial Fellow, King's Fund Policy Institute

In trying to decide what topic to address as my contribution to this volume of essays, I found myself somewhat perplexed. It should be a topic of interest to Robert Maxwell, for sure, but using this criterion still left the field wide open. For one of Robert's characteristics is precisely the width of his interests: an openness to ideas, a refusal to dogmatise, even while committed to a set of strong personal ideals.

He has, in his years at the King's Fund, been both Diaghelev and Nijinsky: impresario and performer, the organiser of complex productions as well as a distinguished soloist. And in his Diaghelev role – spotting talent, identifying new issues and intellectual trends and orchestrating ways of exploring these – he has not only helped to shape the agenda of health policy debate but, equally important, provided a platform for many different views. Like all good promoters of debate, he has encouraged variety – bringing together different, sometimes conflicting perspectives, rather than seeking to achieve unanimity or impose conformity.

In deciding my topic I therefore decided to take my cue from my own occasional contributions to these debates. In the early 1980s Robert edited two collections of essays[1,2] which addressed, in different ways, the issue of public participation in health care policy. Not only was this a good example of Robert's acuity in spotting emergent issues: public participation has now again surfaced as a major policy concern, with much talk about the 'democratic deficit'[3] in the NHS. But the fact that I was invited to contribute to both these collections also underlined Robert's tolerance – indeed encouragement – of dissenting voices: my own rather sceptical views were at odds not just with the prevailing consensus but, I suspect, also with Robert's own position. So in this essay I address the question of whether there is indeed a 'democratic deficit' – a phrase, as I shall argue, which is as vacuous as it is popular – and, if so, what could or should be done about it.

First, some ground clearing. 'Democracy,' as Bernard Crick pointed out a long time ago, 'is perhaps the most promiscuous word in the world of public affairs'.[4] It is a catch-all notion – designed to evoke praise or blame rather than to promote thought – which needs unbundling. Government by elected representatives – with a periodic chance to throw the rascals out – may be a necessary condition. But it is far from a sufficient one: there are plenty of examples of elected tyrannies. 'I have never believed that the demands of democracy are necessarily satisfied merely by the opportunity of putting a cross against someone's name every four or five years,' Aneurin Bevan told the House of Commons when introducing his National Health

Service Bill in 1946. 'I believe that democracy exists in the active participation in administration and policy'.[5]

The proposition that democracy involves 'active participation' does not, however, necessarily get us very far, as Bevan's own invocation of it demonstrates. Bevan used the phrase not in order to argue for public involvement in the running of the NHS (which is what nowadays we might think he meant), but in order to justify his decision to give the medical profession 'full participation in the administration of their own profession'. Indeed the NHS, as designed by him, gave singularly little opportunity for public participation: a crucial point, which is further developed below. So to talk about 'participation' does not necessarily get us very far: it begs the question of participation by whom and how. Participation, on closer examination, turns out to be almost as promiscuous a term as democracy, evoking a cosy vision of Athenian citizens, but not of course women or slaves, meeting in a body to decide their city's policies (a vision unclouded by the fact that these decisions, as even a casual reading of Thucydides or Plato shows, often ended in disaster).

So we are still left groping as we struggle to define what we mean when we invoke the word 'democracy'. Following Crick, I would suggest that it is essentially 'a style of politics or rule': that the criteria for assessing particular institutional or constitutional arrangements are whether or not they promote the achievement of a society in which citizens can call their governors to account, are protected against arbitrary decisions and have the opportunity to influence policy-making (either as individuals or as members of groups). Democracy, in short, implies a particular way of doing things: pluralistic debate, transparency in decision-making, responsiveness to the views of citizens and the availability of information – for how can there be accountability or debate without adequate information? And if we want to know whether there is a 'democratic deficit' in the way in which the NHS is run, it is these specific criteria that we should use.

The case of the NHS

In applying these criteria to the NHS, we are faced with a puzzle. This is that the rhetoric of a 'democratic deficit' has emerged at a time when the NHS has moved nearer to satisfying most of the criteria than at any time in its history. In what follows, I will try to justify this assertion as well as discussing whether it has moved far enough. But, first, some history. The NHS, as originally conceived, was essentially paternalistic. Given that the aim was to assure 'every citizen in this country the same standard of service,' as Bevan put it when introducing his Bill, then there had to be a national, Exchequer-funded system. Given also that the aim was to diffuse the benefits of medical science, 'the voice of the expert', to quote Bevan again,[6] had to be given a large role in the running of the service. Given finally that the aim was to achieve an effective distribution of health care facilities, it had to be organised on a regional rather than local basis.[7] The imperatives of technical efficiency, in short, trumped all other considerations, all the more so since they appeared to be in accord with the requirements of social justice and the strong antagonism of the medical profession towards a local government-based system of health care.

So, from the start – and uniquely among the advanced industrialised countries of the world – Britain had a 'centralised' (Bevan's own phrase) health care system. It represented, as it were, the apotheosis of expertise. True, there were regional boards and local hospital management committees. But their members were nominated (directly or indirectly) by the Minister. As one Labour backbench MP complained during the debate on the Bill: 'What the Minister has done is to say, "I am the final arbitrator in deciding who shall man every stage of administration" ... Why this loss of faith in the elective principle? Why this loss of faith in what we believe to be democracy?' And Bevan himself, in a paper to the Cabinet, defined the role of the various boards and committees as follows: 'They will be the agents (though not, I hope, in any derogatory sense the creatures) of my Department'.[8]

Nor could it be otherwise. Enter the doctrine of Parliamentary accountability. Given a service funded by the Exchequer, the Minister (later Secretary of State) for Health was answerable to Parliament for the NHS: a function which clearly he could only perform if, in turn, any subordinate boards or committees were answerable to him. From this flowed the bedpan doctrine as defined by Bevan: 'When a bed-pan is dropped on a hospital floor, its noise should resound in the Palace of Westminster'.[9] Although successive Secretaries of State – Conservative and Labour – have stressed the need to devolve decision-making, to make the delivery of health care responsive to local circumstances, the doctrine of public accountability has invariably dragged them back into asserting control. The history of the NHS is, in this respect, a manic-depressive cycle of devolution followed by renewed centralisation.

What this potted history suggests is that much of the debate about 'democracy' in the NHS begs the question about where the locus of decision-making should be: the appropriate division of responsibility between centre and periphery. In turn, this prompts the further, and crucial, question of what the limits of tolerable diversity are: what kinds of variations in service provision are acceptable. If the aim continues to be to assure 'every citizen in this country the *same* [my emphasis] standard of service' – and, as it is being increasingly argued, to assure also access to the same package of health care – then central direction is inevitable. If, however, we see the NHS as a conglomerate of local health services with varying standards and offering different packages, then clearly there is scope also for local discretion in policy-making and the question of who should exercise such discretion, and how, comes to the forefront.

It is the failure to face up to, let alone resolve, these issues that largely explains, I suspect, the sense of malaise that has produced the 'democratic deficit' rhetoric. That, plus the decline of deference towards expertise as represented by the medical profession. In a sense the NHS has made the worst of both worlds: it combines a high degree of centralisation with a considerable degree of variation in access to different types of services. More than 50 years after Bevan set out his aim as being 'to provide the people of Great Britain, no matter where they may be, with the same level of service', the NHS has failed to achieve this: very considerable progress towards achieving geographical equity in funding has not brought about uniformity in the mix and level of services provided. Increasingly, the media are drawing attention to the large variations in access to services, whether *in vitro* fertilisation or abortion, and the availability of expensive new drugs.

In the past such variations tended to be seen as a technical challenge rather than as an issue of governance: raising questions about the efficient use of resources and the measurement of need rather than about the local decision-making processes that have produced them. If there is disquiet now, it is because variations are no longer seen as technical issues but as raising the fundamental political question of who gets what and how such decisions are or should be made.

So I come to the main theme of this essay. In the case of the central direction of the service, as I shall argue, we have to a large extent succeeded in creating the requisites of a democratic style of governance. It is in the local administration of the service and in the legitimation of local variations, if that is what we want, that there appear to be deficiencies. Taking the argument one step further (and perhaps one step too far) it is tempting to argue that the overdevelopment of democracy at the centre has led to the underdevelopment of democracy at the periphery. In the following two sections, I elaborate on each of these points in turn.

Opening up the centre

Given that the NHS is indeed a centralised service, the key question, surely, is whether the style of governance at the centre meets the criteria set out at the beginning of this essay. Is there adequate accountability? Is there adequate information? Does the system of decision making allow for the competing interests in the health care arena to participate in the decision making process? Is there an appropriate degree of sensitivity to the concerns of individuals and groups?

In the case of accountability, the answer seems reasonably clear-cut. The bed-pan doctrine still lives. The Secretary of State remains, in effect, answerable to Parliament for everything that happens in the NHS. In any one year, the Department of Health is likely to deal with 3000-plus Parliamentary Questions – more than any other Whitehall Department – and getting on for 60,000 letters from the public.[10] If anything, the problem here is one of 'accountability overload' on ministers and civil servants: it has been estimated that the staff of the NHS Executive spend something like 75 or 80 per cent of their time on ministerial and parliamentary business.[11] For each question and each letter require the civil servants to delve into what is happening at the periphery.

But, more important, Parliament's ability to scrutinise what is happening in the NHS has greatly improved since Bevan's day. Here the most significant development has been the emergence of the Health Committee, with its annual review of public spending plans and *ad hoc* inquiries into specific issues. This is in addition to the powerful Public Accounts Committee. Together the two committees direct a powerful searchlight of publicity on the affairs of the NHS.

The precise meaning of parliamentary accountability has provoked a great deal of debate.[12] Ministers, the Government has argued, are accountable to Parliament for everything that happens in their departments, in the sense that they are answerable for what has happened: i.e. they must provide an explanation. But they are not necessarily 'responsible': i.e. it does not follow they will carry any personal blame. Ministerial resignations are therefore much rarer than policy fiascos, and the relative contribution of politicians and civil servants to such fiascos remains shrouded in secrecy. In short, the power of Parliament lies in its ability to shame or embarrass ministers, whose reactions to parliamentary criticism will largely depend on the thickness of their skins, rather than to exact retribution for failure in performance. In any case, since many parliamentary inquiries are retrospective, the minister concerned may well have moved on.

However, if we think that informed debate is one of the defining characteristics of a democratic style of governance, then clearly parliamentary committees play an important role. Their reports (and even more so, the volumes of evidence that accompany them) provide an invaluable source of information for anyone wanting to understand what is going on in the NHS. If the conclusions that committees draw tend to be unremarkable – given the pressure to avoid party conflict among their members – this does not diminish their role in giving visibility to what is happening in the NHS. However, their experience does suggest a depressing conclusion for those of us who believe that visibility and transparency are key elements in a democratic style of governance: making more information available does not necessarily guarantee that it will be used. My own disillusioned judgement (as a sometime special adviser) is that the information generated by parliamentary committees is massively underused: that it becomes academic fodder rather than material for public debate – which may tell us something about the way in which the media handle complex policy issues.

There is clearly scope for strengthening the capacity of parliamentary committees to scrutinise the activities of government. At present they are served by parliamentary clerks and special advisers recruited for specific inquiries. It is these who are responsible for preparing the ground and drafting the questions to be put to ministers and civil servants giving evidence. It is a method of inquiry biased in favour of those giving evidence, since the questioning is done on the principle that every committee member must have a turn (even if these have only a hazy notion of what the inquiry is about or are intent on pursuing personal obsessions).

One improvement therefore might be for committees to appoint – on the model of the US Congress – a parliamentary counsel to do the cross-examination. Similarly, there is a case for committees to build up a larger, more expert staff. However, this carries the danger of duplicating – at considerable expense – departmental expertise. A better solution might be for committees to draw more on the expertise of existing bodies: so, for example, the Health Committee might build up a regular relationship with the King's Fund Policy

Institute (which in the past has provided specialist advisers for particular inquiries).

There is a further possibility, which is to use the Audit Commission to strengthen parliamentary accountability. The Audit Commission is the loose cannon in the armoury of NHS accountability. Originally created to audit local government, its remit was extended in 1991 to cover the NHS. Since then it has produced a series of wide-ranging and highly informative national surveys – on management costs in the NHS, the performance of fundholders and the organisation of specific clinical services, among many others – quite apart from its work in auditing NHS authorities and trusts. But its constitution reflects its origins in local government: its work is directed by its own, independent board. Hence the case for giving the House of Commons Health Committee a role in determining the Audit Commission's work programme for the NHS and using its reports as the raw material for its own inquiries, in much the same way as the Public Accounts Committee is serviced by the National Audit Office.

The emergence of the Audit Commission as a powerful player in the health care field is one piece of evidence to substantiate my assertion that, contrary to the 'democratic deficit' thesis, there has actually been an increase in our ability to scrutinise, inform ourselves and debate what is happening in the NHS. Other examples might be cited: for instance, the remit of the Health Service Commissioner has been widened to include clinical matters.

All this, it might however be argued, is the small change of governance (though the ability to seek redress is crucial for individual citizens). What is the point of having more information if there is no opportunity to deploy it on crucial issues, if policy is the product not of pluralistic debate but of government diktats? The case of the 1991 NHS reforms would seem to make the point. In this instance, Mrs Thatcher – like Bevan in 1948 – bulldozed her reforms through Parliament, ignoring all outside opposition. In this instance, too, Mrs Thatcher – again like Bevan in 1948 – was accused of refusing to consult, either before or after producing her plans. The similarities are striking and underline the fact that both sets of legislation were exceptional in that they represented attempts to introduce fundamental change in the constitution of health care.[13] They are therefore limiting cases, at the outer boundary of normal policy-making. If there was a widespread sense of outrage, it was precisely because those responsible were felt to be breaking the normal conventions, of acting as an 'elective tyranny', rather than seeking to reconcile conflicting and competing interests. And in both cases, there was a subsequent return to a more accommodating, inclusive style of policy-making.

Indeed, in some respects at least, the existing style of decision-making at the centre remains, if anything, too accommodating, too respectful of special interests. The medical profession may have lost its ability to veto policy, not least because of Mrs Thatcher's demonstration of its impotence in the confrontation over the 1991 reforms. But greater pluralism – greater openness to various views and pressures – may have its own pathologies. For example, in the case of hospital closures, ministers continue to show themselves extraordinarily sensitive to constituency interests and professional pressures. Which suggests that 'democracy' in action may evoke ambivalent reactions: we are all in favour of open discussion, the involvement of all the interests concerned and sensitivity to public opinion, but tend to complain (when we do not like the outcomes of deliberation) about the excessive influence of particular groups or the refusal of politicians to take unpopular decisions. There are many publics with conflicting interests – some better organised to make their views heard than others – and the political process of seeking an accommodation is far from easy.

The decision-making process at the centre could and should, of course, be further improved to bring it into greater conformity with the criteria for our desired style of governance. The promised Freedom of Information Act will help, though we should not perhaps expect too much from access to even more information than we can cope with already. So, too, would implementing the long-advocated proposal for pre-legislative hearings by parliamentary committees, where evidence and argument would be presented before the Government sets its own ideas in the concrete of a Bill.

But none of the changes discussed in this section would deal with what is emerging, as I have argued, as the central dilemma of governance and some of them would indeed make it even more acute. The more we strengthen the machinery for scrutinising the activities of the NHS from the centre – in the name of accountability, openness and all the other hurrah words of democracy – the greater becomes the problem of giving meaning to these same concepts at the local level.

Peripheral visions

One of characteristics of the post-1991 era in the history of the NHS is the mass conversion of the authorities at the periphery to the notion of public involvement.[14] It is, of course, a conversion made all the easier by the fact that the notion of public involvement is, itself, so fuzzy and elastic that it is capable of many interpretations. Spurred on by central government, purchasing authorities have engaged in a ferment of activity designed to elicit local voices: surveys, focus groups, discussion forums and citizens' juries are now routine features of the NHS landscape at the local level. It is an open question of how far this sort of activity affects the decision-making process, as distinct from helping to provide evidence in support of decisions already made: the boundaries between involving and manipulating the public may often be blurred. Nevertheless, the very fact that there is now increasingly a perceived need to ground decisions in public consent and the acceptance that the language of expertise has no monopoly in the decision-making process represent a major shift, inconceivable even ten years ago.

At the same time (to return to our criteria of a democratic style of governance), there has been a very considerable increase in the flow of information to the public since 1991: a trickle has become an avalanche. Commissioning authorities have to publish their purchasing plans, setting out their priorities (an obligation which, however, is about to be scrapped by the new Government: an unfortunate retreat from openness). The management letters of the Audit Commission's auditors, analysing the finances and activities of both commissioning authorities and trusts, are notionally private documents but in practice are made available under the Code of Openness.[14] Central government publishes a performance guide, showing how individual providers perform against the Citizen's Charter benchmarks. Indicators of clinical performance are now in the pipeline.

Much of this information is problematic. Purchasing plans tend to be idiosyncratic documents, not always easy to decode: there is a strong case for standardising the format in which they are presented (so once again we are back to calling for greater direction from the centre). The management letters of the auditors, too, require some sophisticated reading between the lines. And the various performance indicators – including the new clinical ones[15] – need a great deal of interpretation. In the NHS, few statistics speak with a clear, unambiguous voice: much debate is a battle to give specific meanings to particular figures or 'facts'.

Even allowing for such reservations, the central puzzle remains: why all these improvements have been accompanied by growing concern about a 'democratic deficit'. So we turn to the other side of the balance sheet. Clearly, fundholding poses major problems of public accountability: those registered with GPs have few opportunities to exercise either voice or exit, and fundholders themselves have only limited obligations to give transparency to their activities and policies. Similarly, there is some ambiguity about the position of trusts. In theory commissioning authorities should hold them accountable for the services they deliver through the contracting process, while they are directly accountable to the Secretary of State for their financial and strategic management. In practice, it is not self-evident that either chain of accountability works effectively.

Above all, of course, there is the question of the composition of the health authorities themselves. The Thatcher reforms carried through the principles enunciated by Aneurin Bevan to their logical consequence. Bevan, let us recall, saw local boards or committees as the 'agents' of central government, explicitly repudiating the notion that they should be in any sense representative. In practice, this principle subsequently became blurred, as both professional interests and local authorities gained rights of representation. The 1991 reforms, replacing members by non-executive directors, thus can be seen simply as an exercise in cutting through ambiguity. Given that the NHS *is* a centralised institution, then the logic is to have at the periphery men and women who are the creatures – in a non-pejorative sense – of the minister. For how, if there is not a hierarchy of managerial command, can the Secretary of State otherwise fulfil his obligations of accountability to Parliament? And if the Secretary of State is not so accountable, in the fullest sense, how can we talk about 'democracy' in the governance of the NHS? Such accountability may not capture all the dimensions of 'democracy' but it is surely the necessary foundation stone for any architecture of governance which can claim to satisfy the other necessary criteria in a national, tax-funded service like the NHS.

Nothing much will change if a Labour Secretary of State replaces one set of non-executive directors with another, or reverts to a more 'representative' system of membership. The notion that someone elected to a local authority thereby gains all-purpose representative legitimacy is decidedly odd; he or she is not going to be voted out of office because of their performance as health authority members. Indeed the evidence suggests that nominated members, precisely because they have no independent authority, tend to see themselves more accountable to their communities than elected ones:[16] hence perhaps the anxiety to engage with the public which has followed the 1991 reforms.

There are other policy options. The role of community health councils could be strengthened. The increase in the availability of information suggests the need, also, for strengthening the capacity to process and interpret what is being produced if the investment is not to go to waste: the amount (and complexity) of information has long since swamped the ability of individual citizens to digest it.

But it is difficult to resist the conclusion that all such measures – however desirable in themselves – would tackle the perception of a 'democratic deficit'. For the very invocation of the phrase suggests that there was a time when there was a 'democratic balance' in the NHS. And the aim of this essay has been to suggest that any such interpretation rests on a false reading of the past. If democracy in the NHS is all about effective central accountability at the centre, then it has never been in a better state than at present. If it is more than that, if it involves a different relationship between centre and periphery, then a more radical approach might well be needed.

Some radical options

The NHS is a creature of its time. It was designed in an era of faith in strong central government, planning by experts and national solutions. That era has gone. We have moved into an era of devolution and consumerism, where governments of all parties are anxious to stress the limits of their ability to shape society and where individuals are increasingly putting together their own welfare packages.[17] In the specific case of health care, we have moved from an era where the emphasis was on meeting need as defined by experts to one in which demands are increasingly being articulated by consumers. Hence the tensions noted in this essay. Hence, too, the case for thinking in terms of changing 'democratic expectations' rather than a 'democratic deficit'; for asking whether a different model of organising health care would meet the criticisms and demands that now appear to be emerging.

One alternative model, which may well be seized upon by the Conservative Party in Opposition, is the democracy of the marketplace in which the consumer is (in theory at least) sovereign. Mrs Thatcher's 1991 reforms stopped well short of embracing this approach, advocated by Enthoven.[18] But it would not be difficult to develop a model in which consumers can choose between competing health plans, which in turn purchase from competing providers, but which yet provides universal, comprehensive health care: something like the Dutch or German systems. Such a model raises a number of objections: the administrative costs involved, the problem of avoiding adverse selection, the restrictive nature of democracy as defined by consumer choice and so on. But lack of feasibility is not among them.

Alternatively, there is the model rejected in 1948: devolving responsibility for running health care to local government. In effect, this would mean adopting the Scandinavian model of health care. The case for so doing has long been argued by David Hunter, John Stewart and others. There remains reason for scepticism. There is little evidence that local authorities provide more responsive – let alone more efficient or effective – services than national organisations. Further, to the extent that local authorities have moved towards a more open style of governance, with more information for the public, it has been under pressure from central government. Local elections tend to be referenda about the performance of national governments, not verdicts on the performance of local councillors. But if we think that centralisation is in itself undesirable, if we think that devolving responsibility to a level of government nearer to the citizen is an aim to be pursued in its own right, then these considerations will tilt the balance of the argument towards the local authority model. And in the specific case of health care, we may further conclude that the experience of the past 50 years has greatly weakened Bevan's central argument for a national system – that only so could local variations in the pattern and level of services be eliminated.

The arguments remain finely balanced. It may be a mistake to exaggerate the extent that public opinion (as distinct from some élite opinion) has become converted to the cause of devolution and decentralisation: increasing central government control over schools has not mobilised crowds in the streets protesting against this attack on local authority autonomy but, on the contrary, appears to be popular. Above all, local government – as at present constituted – lacks the financial resources to take on health care: simply to transfer the present NHS budget to local authorities would divorce funding from accountability.

So for the time being, there may be a case for some modest experiments designed to satisfy at least some of the changing 'democratic expectations'. Local authorities could be given a statutory right to raise extra rates to supplement the local health care budget: what might be called the Scottish model. If the local population puts a higher value on access to a local hospital than the national calculus (and a lower weight, perhaps, on the possible risks), then why not allow them to put their money behind their voice? Again, local authorities might be given a statutory responsibility to review the performance, reports and accounts of the health authorities, trusts and fundholders in their area: in other words, they could carry out the same function as the House of Commons Health Committee.

However, the notion of changing 'democratic expectations' needs to be treated with the same scepticism – and disaggregated – as the notion of a 'democratic deficit'. There is, clearly, an increasing demand among individual patients for a greater say in the way they are treated: for greater respect for their autonomy. There is, similarly, evidence that specific groups of consumers – in particular those with continuing needs – want to be involved in planning the way the services for them are organised and delivered. It is not self-evident, however, that there is a frustrated demand among citizens in general – as distinct from groups representing particular interests – for greater involvement in the affairs of the NHS. This is an assumption that requires testing.

References

1. Maxwell RJ, Morrison V (eds). *Working with people*. London: King Edward's Hospital Fund for London, 1983.
2. Maxwell RJ, Weaver N (eds). *Public participation in health*. London: King Edward's Hospital Fund for London, 1984.
3. Coote A. The democratic deficit. In: Marinker M (ed). *Sense and sensibility in health care*. London: BMJ Publishing Group, 1996, pp.173–97.
4. Crick B. *In defence of politics*. Harmondsworth: Penguin, 1964.
5. Bevan A. *National Health Service Bill: second reading debate*. London: Hansard, 1946, 5th series, Vol.422, Cols.43–63.
6. *The future of the hospital services: memorandum by the Minister of Health*. CP(45) 205, 5 October 1945. London: Public Records Office, CAB 129.
7. Fox DM. *Health policies, health politics*. Princeton (NJ): Princeton University Press, 1986.
8. *The hospital services: memorandum by the Minister of Health*. CP(45) 231 16 October 1945. London: Public Records Office, CAB 129.
9. Quoted in Nairne P. Parliamentary control and accountability. In: Maxwell RJ, Weaver N, *op.cit.*, pp.33–50.

10. Banks T et al. *Review of the wider Department of Health*. London: Department of Health, 1994.
11. Day P, Klein R. *Steering but not rowing? The transformation of the DoH: a case study*. Bristol: The Policy Press, 1997.
12. Treasury and Civil Service Committee. *The role of the Civil Service*. Fifth Report Session 1993–94. London: HMSO, HC 27.
13. Day P, Klein R. Constitutional and distributional conflict in British medical politics. *Political Studies* 1992; XL:462–78.
14. Dixon J, Klein R. It's all in the balance. *Health Service Journal* 1997; 5 June, pp.26–27.
15. McKee M. Indicators of clinical performance. *British Medical Journal* 1997; 19 July, p.142.
16. Day P, Klein R. *Accountabilities: five public services*. London: Tavistock Publications, 1997.
17. Klein R, Millar J. Do-it-yourself social policy: searching for a new paradigm. *Social Policy & Administration* 1995; 29(4):303–16.
18. Enthoven AC. *Reflections on the management of the National Health Service*. London: The Nuffield Provincial Hospitals Trust, 1985.

The future of primary health care

Marshall Marinker OBE
Visiting Professor, United Medical and Dental Schools
of Guy's and St Thomas', University of London

It is a pleasure to be asked to contribute to this Festschrift for Robert Maxwell. I was invited by the editors to consider the future of primary health care. Because of my background and limitations, I am going to look at this future from the point of view and prejudice of what I still think of as general medical practice.

As will become evident, this terminological preference is more than a petulant and geriatric affectation. It is a comment on the historical transience of the concept of 'primary' health care, and an argument for the more enduring relevance of the 'general' practice of medicine.

I will begin by describing the development of some of the key ideas of general practitioners, over the past five decades. In this, although the description will have something of caricature in its brief outlines, the power of charismatic individuals and fashionable movements will be seen to produce serious consequences. Rudolph Klein has spoken about changing health service policy as 'fads and fashions', and this is echoed in the unfolding of clinical concepts in general practice. Next, I will examine what is happening to the words that we use when we talk about health policy. In this, the contingency of our ideas will suggest that not all our current meanings will survive in the health service to come. Lastly, I will venture one or two tentative predictions, which may, of course, also be read as wishes or warnings in transparent disguise.

Clinical fashions

The early years of the NHS saw a burgeoning of new thinking about the context and tasks of general practice. Reading Stephen Taylor's classic *Good general practice*[1] reveals something of the tensions between the medicine of the teaching hospitals, still charged with the task of producing the 'safe practitioner', and the experience of general practitioners responding to illness 'out there', far from the seeming certainties of the radiology department and the post-mortem room. But Taylor's survey and apologia scarcely hint at the rapidly changing meanings that would soon be attached to the general practitioners' ideas about 'what is wrong'.

The periods in which these ideas were most fashionable appear as geological strata, discernible in the unearthing of how general practitioners came to think about 'what is wrong' with the patient.[2] The first stratum is epidemiology. Public health academics such as Maurice Backet were measuring workload and perceived morbidities in general practice. General practitioners such as John Fry were recording the natural histories that longitudinal care, built into the structure of NHS general practice, now revealed. Although expressed in quantitative terms, this was nothing less revolutionary than '*the diagnosis as narrative*'. Among the first general practitioners to estimate incidence and prevalence and outcome was a rural practitioner from Redcar in Yorkshire. Hodgkin's study remains a landmark of enduring significance. In his preface he writes, 'Any service to a community has two conflicting components: the standard of service delivered to the individual; the standard of service delivered to the group as a whole'.[3] The working out of this unresolvable conflict dominated the concepts of general practice throughout the history of the NHS.

One of the deepest strata is '*the illness as patient*', the notion that the patient, and not just the disease, is the prime object of the doctor's enquiry. It was the work of Michael Balint's training-cum-research seminars in the 1950s and 1960s that established 'the patient as diagnosis'.[4] Others then urged the extension of the doctor's enquiry beyond the individual to the domestic group. The long-established term 'family medicine', which McWhinney[5] preferred to 'general practice' on marketing grounds, was elevated to a philosophy of care. This movement was stronger in the USA than in the UK, but a new awareness of the psycho-social dimensions of the clinical task resulted in the notion of '*the patient as family, and the family as illness*'.[6, 7, 8]

The next stratum marks a shift back to objectifying the clinical task. Although originating in the hospital-based teaching of transatlantic medical schools, Laurence Weed's introduction of disciplined medical record-keeping[9] marked a renewed attempt to obliterate the patient's story of the illness as told in the patient's own language. It was finally to be replaced with a new narrative convention – the medical detective story or problem-oriented medical record. '*The diagnosis as puzzle*', and the diagnostic task as puzzle-solving (misleadingly described as problem-solving), survives in the present construction of the clinical notes and has its latest manifestation in the computerised records of the 1990s.

The next archaeological layer reveals 'the diagnosis as risk'. This was the extension of 'what is wrong' from time past and present time, where it had traditionally been sought, into the future. Beguiled by the belief, or at least the wish, that most diagnosis is best made as early as possible in its natural history, general practitioners became preoccupied with the medicalising of the still well. A certain American academic (I cannot positively identify him) is credited with the absolute definition: 'a healthy person is someone who has been inadequately investigated by a physician'. Reports from the Royal College of General Practitioners[10] urged prevention. The fine but critical distinction between being a person and being a patient became obliterated in this swirling tide of well intentioned, but not always well-judged, iatric imperialism.

Nearer the contemporary surface of the 1990s NHS, the resolution of the dilemma between individual and population that Hodgkin[3] described, seemed to tilt in favour of populations. Epidemiological evidence had long and overwhelmingly implicated poverty, and its concomitants, as the major factor associated with excess morbidity and premature mortality. The Black Report[11] in 1980 underscored Julian Tudor Hart's[12] claim in 1971 that those in greatest need of health care because of their socio-economic situation were least provided for. The patient, in Hart's language, had become the population, and the clinical task, the prevention of illness on a population scale: this was 'the illness as community'. Hart talked of 'the fusion of epidemiology with primary care'.[13]

As I write, the surface of this archaeological dig is characterised by other values. The clinical implications of contemporary cost-benefit and similar analyses from health economics have resulted in a further redefinition of 'what is wrong'. The calculations of quality-adjusted life years (QUALYS), and the guidelines implied by the electronic digestion of randomised controlled trials, have given us 'the illness as commodity'. These are the commodities that are traded in the internal markets introduced in 1990.

Words and meanings

The North American philosopher Richard Rorty[14] says that we use language in order to create metaphors by which we manipulate the world in which we find ourselves. In other words the so-called reality of health and health care is created and limited by the language that we have been taught to use. Reality is made by our words, and words are not given, we continually remake them. And, says Rorty, all words are contingent, are relative. They are relative to the environment which they describe, control and change.

All the words that describe our present institutions of health care, and the roles of the health care professional, are fraying at the edges. In a living language that is what happens to words. In his poem *Burnt Norton* TS Eliot writes:

> Words strain,
> Crack and sometimes break, under the burden,
> Under the tension, slip, slide, perish,
> Decay with imprecision, will not stay in place,
> Will not stay still.[15]

The pace of contemporary change in the NHS seems without precedent. So consider what is happening to the current meaning of some of our much used words.

Recently, in the course of an enquiry into the problems that patients experience with medicine-taking,[16] I heard evidence from a patient who required maintenance therapy following renal transplantation some years ago. His medication regimen was complex and addressed a variety of therapeutic intentions, many of them geared to redressing the insults to his system caused by the immunosuppressant drugs which were essential in warding off rejection. He said that he needed continuity of care, but something additional to the continuity of *personal* care that was the major characteristic of his general practice. He needed the continuity of *specialist* expertise that he found only among the doctors and nurses of his renal unit. What he did *not* need were the boundary disputes about day-to-day responsibility for the monitoring of his condition or the cost of the drug budget.

The primary/secondary care division, the very basis of our NHS, was a San Andreas fault that threatened the management of this man's problems.

It was not the hospital or the consultant or the health centre or the general practitioner that he saw as the locus of care: it was the specialist renal unit team, a sort of micro-*Medicins sans Frontières*. It was a team located not in 'the hospital' or in 'the community', but in a new sort of 'health care continuum'. This was a team in which he was required to perform as an active member. And it functioned in a space that sometimes resembled a war-torn no-man's land.

Nowadays, the meaning of the word 'hospital' changes from year to year, and from location to location. Day surgery, outreach programmes, hospitals in the home, consultation by telemedicine are transforming our hospitals from clinical hotels into technical resource centres. The general hospital is a concept that cannot long resist the growing evidence of a linear relationship between volume of specialised cases treated and quality of treatment outcome. Specialist treatments will become increasingly industrialised.

Patients are increasingly informed. They are encouraged, for example by charters and consumerist organisations, to regard the relationship with doctors as a matter of contract rather than trust. The key ethical principles are no longer the doctor's beneficence and non-maleficence, but the patient's autonomy and sense of personal justice. Fed by the medical profession's passions for prevention and risk avoidance, the media are making the public more 'health-conscious'. Consequently, there is a blurring or even an obliteration of the difference between the terms 'patient' and 'person'. Since everyone is now a patient, and charters imply contract, we may be in on the death of the patient–doctor relationship.

Alvin Toffler[17] first drew our attention to the social consequences of the new technologies, and predicted that our society would become increasingly heterogeneous, sustaining a large variety of micro-communities. The UK may soon divide on more than old pre-union or regional lines, and we may well see new dimensions of identity and loyalty. This could happen because, in addition to, and alongside, geographical communities, the internet makes possible the creation of 'virtual communities' based on other characteristics than neighbourhood or patriotism – for example having common values and tastes or shared problems, like suffering from the same diseases.

Medicine is already characterised by the escalating costs of its biotechnical inventions; by the blurring of clear differences between well and ill; between live and dead, human and non-human. Technical mastery is redefining the boundaries between health and pleasure: new treatments will sooner or later offer the chemical reconstruction of the personality, and the surgical and pharmacological remodelling of the body. Cosmetic surgeons already offer us improved, or at least socially approved, appearance. Psychiatry embraces the medicalisation of socio-pathic behaviour and social deviance. When the pharmaceutical industry introduces drugs able to enhance our 'normal' mood, to increase our retentive memories, to enrich our sensations and so on, they will move from being a health care industry, to becoming a life-enhancement industry. Will medicine, and the NHS, follow?

Genomics changes the basis of diagnosis and prognosis from what it has always been in the past – a probabilistic judgement based only on large-group data, to become something much more threatening – a personally predictive medicine. Genetic engineering is transforming not only our concept of inheritance and risk, but (as the recent news of the cloning of Dolly the sheep suggested) our very concept of self. Information technology will drive the most profound changes of all. We can already see the early outlines of an international, accessible, transparent and total health-and-medical information machine on the internet. It will be shared by the health professionals, managers and by the public – with input from research, from performance data and from patients themselves (with web sites, bulletin boards, and electronic cafés or cyberclinics on locations that had once been health centres). The patient's central personal records will no longer be located in the doctors' filing cabinets, but electronically on patient-held smart cards (with 'healthpoint readers' in surgery and outpatient waiting rooms, in chemists' shops and shopping malls).

I have suggested something of the transparency, transience and contingency of concepts that once looked solid and permanent – both in the doctor's concept of 'what is wrong' and in the structures and functions of the NHS. How can a sound future of health care be built from such fragile material?

Imaginizations

In his monograph *Images of organisations* Gareth Morgan[18] describes the pervasive power of metaphor on our lives. Metaphor is intrinsic to the developed use of language. It allows us to see one reality as though it were another. It disrupts expectation and experience with fresh perspectives, it springs the surprises that constitute the discoveries of science and the novelties of art. The exploration of metaphor forms a central tool in the contemporary analysis of art, linguistics, theoretical physics, psychoanalytical theory, social theory and much else. Morgan's contribution was to apply these method of metaphorical analysis to the theory of organisations.

Morgan develops an interesting taxonomy. For example, his first image is the very familiar one of the organisation as 'machine', with its emphasis on central control, explicit rules, rigid discipline, uniformity, specialisation and predictability. This was, he argued, still the dominant model.

Another intriguing metaphor is the organisation as 'psychic prison'. Here the members are constantly trapped by archaic memories of the organisation's real or imagined history. Many general practices, as well as our great teaching hospitals, seem rather like that. Drawing on Jungian imagery, Morgan suggests that such organisational life can be understood in terms of the relationship between fools, magicians, warriors, high priests, lovers and other symbolic characters. Recently, a think-tank of very senior public health professionals, contemplating their positions as newly corporate members of health authorities and trusts, identified one of the key roles of the directors public health as that of 'poet in residence'.[19]

The most intriguing of Morgan's metaphors is the organisation as 'bio-organism'. This is characterised by a concern to preserve the internal environment, while at the same time discovering ecological niches, capitalising on natural advantage, continuously interacting with, and adapting to, the changing external environment. But Morgan points out that we are free to invent our own images of organisation. For this fusion between organisation and imagination, Morgan coined the term 'imaginization'. Imaginization suggests that we can perpetually re-invent our professional organisations and our health care system.

To build alternative futures requires, first, a willingness to entertain a demolition of what no longer seems to serve its original purpose and, second, the creativity to imagine something more appropriate to the age. Demolition requires little more than a fresh examination of the assumptions, the baggage we carry from a past no longer relevant to new times. General practice evolved from the work of apothecaries and surgeons in the mid-18th century. Its place in the matrix of health care resulted in the referral system. This was a restrictive practices deal hammered out between those who were to be called general practitioners and would abjure the right to practise in hospitals and physicians and surgeons, who would henceforward alone have the right to hospital practice. These physicians and surgeons would only see patients when consulted by general practitioners. They thus became consultants. In terms of professional etiquette it is the general practitioner and not the patient who consults the specialist. The phrase 'I will be writing to your doctor' still enshrines this 19th century version of what was essentially an inter-trade-union agreement.

This referral system might well be described as a conspiracy between government and profession to deprive the patient of a civil liberty. Yet in the UK the fact that the patient has almost no direct access to the specialist has seemed acceptable to most of the population. The 'almost' refers to the growing tendency of the privately insured middle class to circumvent the system.

The profession's argument in favour of the referral system[20] has been grounded in the danger of permitting patients to decide what is wrong with them, and in the need to protect them from the excesses of specialist investigation and treatments. All of this is predicated on the assumption of patients' inability to know what their problem is, to know their own mind, and to decide where to look for help. But can these assumptions be sustained?

Information technology may now make possible a truly patient-led service. If continuity of care can reside in the patient-held smart-card (on which patients themselves can write), choice may come to be seen as the benchmark of quality in health care, as in other personal services. An interactive health information machine on the internet, open to professionals and public alike, is already in the making.[21] A new level of participation by patients in their own primary diagnosis seems to be an inevitable consequence. As the public becomes more informed and more discriminating, is it not simply medical hubris to maintain that the patient cannot in the future navigate the health service in some new ways?

Continuity of care has traditionally been seen as the unique province of the general practitioner, and essential for a logical and safe practice. Yet continuity has always been more valued by doctors than by patients, for whom accessibility, listening skills and competence have been the really important desiderata. Increasingly, the profession itself has been questioning the mantra of continuity and seeking to redefine it in terms of team coherence rather than personal 'longitudinal' care.[22] And as teamwork has burgeoned, it has become apparent that in many community-based services clinicians with a nursing background possess superior specialised knowledge and skills and sensitivities in the care of patients with diabetes, with rehabilitation needs following a heart attack or stroke, with mental illness, cancer, and so on. Demolition means jettisoning our past assumptions about the roles of patients, doctors, nurses and others.

Blueprints, my second desideratum, require imaginization. It may entail redesigning the clinical workforce, such that the boundaries between nursing, and medicine, hospital and community are dissolved. When words fray, we need to accept new meanings or invent new words. I am going to limit myself to only one preferred scenario, a piece of imaginization concerning the future of general practitioners. The explanation of this choice, as I confessed at the outset of this essay, must be sought in my personal history: I prefer to envisage the transformation of my colleagues, than to compose their historical *requiescat*.

The key task of all physicians is diagnosis. The diagnostic task of the specialist is to reduce uncertainty, to explore possibility and to marginalise error. For the general practitioner the task is quite different. It is to mediate between the predicament of the individual and the potential of bio-science. It is to tolerate uncertainty, to explore probability and to marginalise danger. If the specialist task is brought to bear on the presentation of every illness, the personal cost in anxiety and distress for the patient, and the economic cost to the service, would be unsustainable. But in the future, patients themselves will be enabled to participate actively in this generalist primary diagnostic task.

As patients assume this more active role, they will need generalist advisers to guide them through choices of diagnosis and treatment. This adviser may have few, if any, directly *therapeutic* responsibilities. These will be in the hands of specialists from both medicine and nursing, or some future amalgamation of both these traditions. The generalist adviser will have the task of translating the increasingly arcane jargon of bio-technology and statistical estimation into the everyday language of the patient.

To fulfil this role, general practitioners must evolve into what I have elsewhere described as personal, or Renaissance, physicians,[23] doctors who will act as overall case managers throughout the clinical pathways of the entire service. The training for this task will include competence in clinical thinking, interpretation of data, the presentation and examination of large moral issues, and sensitivity to the patient's personal biographical values. In this the general practitioner, as personal physician, must become truly a consultant – a doctor consulted by the patient.

Sir Cyril Chantler, Principal at UMDS, has long been sympathetic to this analysis. Recently, he speculated that perhaps before long a clinical career would begin in a specialism, and aspire and progress, in maturity, to the attainment of generalist status.[24] Nor can this new role be confined by outdated demarcations between what we now call 'primary' and 'secondary' care. The patient's personal physician must function across all the arbitrary boundaries of care.

If the organisations of the future that we imaginize behave more like biological organisms than machines, they will be able to adapt to the changing social and epidemiological environments, and they will come to occupy ecological niches in an ever more complex and diverse health service. A health service equitably serving such a diverse society will need strong central commitment to adequate funding and moral purpose. It will also need a greater flexibility and variety of structure and function than we have hitherto thought feasible or desirable.

There will be many other imaginizations, and better ones than I can devise for the purpose of this essay. Market competition seemed, after all, not to fit the ethos of a National Health Service. Competition between different ideas and models may serve us far better. I have argued that these new models cannot necessarily be designed and constructed simply by rearranging the familiar components of our present NHS. Therefore any predictions about the future of primary health care must be based on an oxymoron. They make too many assumptions. The purpose of this essay has been to challenge them.

References
1. Tylor S. *Good general practice*. Oxford: 1952
2. Marinker M. 'What is wrong' and 'How we know it'. In: Loudon D, Horder J, Webster C (eds). *A history of general practice under the NHS*. Oxford: OUP (in press).
3. Hodgkin K. *Towards earlier diagnosis*. Edinburgh: 1963.
4. Balint M. *The doctor, his patient and the illness*. London: 1957.
5. McWhinney IR. General practice as an academic discipline. *Lancet* 1964; 419–23.

6. *Report of the Sub-Committee on the Field of Work of the Family Doctor.* London: 1963.
7. Kellner R. *Family ill health.* London: 1963.
8. Huygen FJA. *Family medicine.* Nijmegen: 1978.
9. Weed LL. *Medical records, medical education, and patient care.* Cleveland: 1969.
10. The Royal College of General Practitioners. Reports from General Practice Nos. 18–21, combined Reports on Prevention. London: 1975.
11. Whitehead M. *The health divide (with the Black Report).* London: 1987.
12. Hart JT. The inverse care law. *Lancet* 1971; 1:405–12.
13 Hart JT. *A new kind of doctor.* London: 1988.
14. Rorty R. *Contingency, irony and solidarity.* Cambridge: 1989.
15. Eliot TS. *The four quartets.* London: 1944.
16. The Royal Pharmaceutical Society of Great Britain. *From compliance to concordance.* London: 1997.
17. Toffler A. *Future shock.* London: 1970.
18. Morgan G. *Images of organisations.* London: 1986.
19. Crown J, Gunning-Scheppers L. The challenge to public health advocacy. In: Marinker M (ed). *Sense and sensibility in health care.* London: 1997.
20. Marinker M. The referral system. *Journal of the Royal College of General Practitioners* 1988; 38:487–91.
21. Spiers J. Jane Austen, hyperspace and patient power. In Marinker M (ed), *op. cit.*
22. Freeman G, Hjortdahl P. What future for continuity of care in general practice? *BMJ* 1997; 314:1870–3.
23. Marinker M. The end of general practice. The 1995 Bayliss Lecture. PPP. London.
24. Chantler C. Personal communication, 1997.

'Regulating' doctors: what makes them practise as they do?

A personal view

Richard Smith
Editor, British Medical Journal

W hat are the forces that determine whether doctors improve their performance or lapse into poor performance or frank misconduct? And how can improvement be encouraged and decay discouraged? These seem to be the central questions to consider in an essay on regulating doctors. They are highly complex questions, and I do not think that I can provide comprehensive answers in a short essay. What I can do is to attempt a broad and subjective view of 'the web of regulation,'(1) paying particular attention to the General Medical Council (GMC), the body most strongly associated with self-regulation by British doctors.

My central thesis is that the bodies traditionally associated with regulation have only a limited impact on how doctors perform. Other forces – particularly internal, cultural ones – have a much stronger influence. My essay on 'regulation' thus pays what many will see as disproportionate attention to influences that are not considered in traditional analyses of regulation.

The multiple forces 'regulating' doctors

What are the forces that determine how doctors perform? Allsop and Mulcahy[1] follow Bosk[2] in suggesting a framework of external and internal, formal and informal forces that regulate doctors' behaviour (Figure 1). This framework is useful for illustrating the many forces

	External	Internal
Formal	NHS	GMC
	Courts	Royal Colleges
	Health Service Commissioner	BMA
	NHS complaints procedures	Other professional organisations
	Employment contracts	Clinical audit
	Government	
	League tables	
Informal	Interaction between public officials and professional leaders	Colleagues
	General media	Professional education
	NHS managers	Medical culture
	Information, through the world wide web	Clinical experience
	Patient organisations	Family
		Pharmaceutical companies
		Medical evidence
		Patients
		Continuing medical education
		Continuing professional development
		Medical press

Figure 1 Forms of 'regulation' of doctors

at play and that the forces that are most often considered in discussions on regulation – the courts and the GMC – may not be the most important. These institutions may have terrible powers at their disposal, including imprisonment and suspension from the medical register, but they are remote. Doctors, as they go about their day-to-day work, will probably not think once of the courts or the GMC, but they are likely to be constantly influenced in their behaviour by colleagues and patients. Regulatory forces might be thought of in terms of power and pervasiveness. The strongest forces will be both powerful and pervasive – like colleagues, particularly those that are bosses. Table 1 shows my judgements on the power and pervasiveness of regulatory forces operating on British doctors and how their influence is changing.

Internal informal regulatory forces

Colleagues and medical culture

If my analysis is right, then the most powerful influences on how doctors practise are concentrated in the internal and informal. Internal can be interpreted as internal to the health service, or internal to the medical profession, or internal to the individual. In Table 1, I use the term to mean internal to the medical profession. It may be that the more internal the influences, the more powerful they are.

Colleagues have a huge influence on how doctors practise. Doctors receive most of their training from other doctors. Medical students and young doctors model themselves on the doctors who teach and impress them. They learn to be sceptical of the teachings and ideas of those who are not doctors. When doctors do not know something, they turn to other doctors, not to books or journals.

Doctors join a tribe – or a priesthood – that has tough initiation rites. The members of the tribe are separated from others by their special knowledge; their familiarity with death, sickness, pain and the intimacies of other peopleÕs lives, minds and bodies; and their special status as healers. Doctors have struck a deal with society.

Table 1 The relative influence of the many forces that influence the practice of doctors

Force	Power	Pervasive-ness	Overall influence (out of 9)	Changing influence
Colleagues (bosses)	High	High	9	Same
Professional education	High	High	9	Same
Medical culture	High	High	9	Same
Clinical experience	High	High	9	Same
Colleagues (equals)	Moderate	High	6	Same
GMC	High	Moderate	6	Up
Employment contracts	High	Moderate	6	Same
Pharmaceutical industry	Moderate	High	6	Same
NHS managers	Moderate	Moderate	4	Up
NHS complaints procedures	Moderate	Moderate	4	Up
Medical evidence	Moderate	Moderate	4	Up
Courts	High	Low	3	Up
Patients	Low	High	3	Up
Colleagues (lower)	Low	High	3	Same
Royal colleges	Moderate	Low	2	Down
Specialist professional organisations	Moderate	Low	2	Up
Continuing professional education/continuing professional development	Low	Moderate	2	Up
Medical press	Low	Moderate	2	Down
Clinical audit	Low	Moderate	2	Up or down
Health Service Commissioner	Moderate	Low	2	Up
General media	Low	Low	1	Same
Interaction between public officials and professional leaders	Low	Low	1	Same
Information for patients – for example, through the world wide web	Low	Low	1	Up
Patients' organisations	Low	Low	1	Up
Explicit ethical codes	Low	Low	1	Up
Explicit professional standards	Low	Low	1	Up

They will grapple with what William Osler – the doctor who is probably quoted more than any other – called 'the perplexity of the soul' in exchange for high status and financial rewards and self-regulation.

The public turns to doctors in moments of extremity and expects an answer, even a solution. Often we cannot provide it. We cannot defeat death, sickness and pain. Everybody within the priesthood knows how vulnerable we are. But the public does not want to know too much about that vulnerability. It hopes we can deliver, and we want to. Indeed, our privileges depend to some extent on us being able to. We are thus permanently conflicted: expected and wanting to deliver but often not being able to.

Among any group the leaders or bosses have great influence – partly through what they say but even more through how they behave. This influence may be especially strong among doctors because of this sense of being apart from the rest of society. Only a neurosurgeon knows how it feels to put a knife into a living brain, and they feel a strong bond with the few other people who have had that experience.

Although doctors have a great influence on each other, they are often fiercely independent. Medicine is a hierarchical profession in that juniors are reluctant to criticise seniors. But once a doctor becomes an independent practitioner (usually at around 30–35), then the ethos is that one doctor is as good as another. Medicine does not have cardinals and bishops. It may have presidents of royal colleges, but their power does not extend to the direct command of independent practitioners. Indeed, doctors are suspicious of those who set themselves up as leaders and are inclined to create unleadable institutions and elect compromise candidates to lead them.[3]

Doctors have a culture of not criticising each other. Rosenthal has attempted to describe the roots of this tendency.[4] Through her ethnographic studies of British doctors she has identified how they practise in a state of 'permanent uncertainty' and must accept that 'fallibility ... [is] an intrinsic part of the practice of medicine'. All doctors have made mistakes, often serious ones, and their experiences 'create a powerful pool of mutual empathy and an unforgettable sense of shared personal vulnerability.' Living this way, doctors are unsurprisingly 'quick to forgive', and 'non-criticism' is the norm. 'Where uncertainty surrounds all members of the profession daily and all see themselves vulnerable to accidents,' writes Rosenthal, 'it is not difficult to understand a tacit norm of non-criticism, a conspiracy of tolerance.'[4]

Doctors also find it difficult to ask each other for help. Proper doctors, like policemen, don't weep. Nor, unlike policemen, do they get sick. Of course, in reality they do, but a recent study showed that three-quarters of doctors would go to work after experiencing a sudden onset headache bad enough to be a cerebral bleed. Medical culture encourages junior doctors to take on more than they can manage and not to ask for help. Repeatedly, confidential inquiries into surgical, obstetric, or medical disasters show that they result from inadequately trained doctors trying to do too much. It is partly that they feel they ought to be able to cope and partly that they are reluctant to call out seniors, especially at night.

I have dwelt on these issues of the influence of colleagues and medical culture because they are, I believe, so powerful. Their power may explain why other more formal and more familiar regulatory forces lack power. NHS complaints procedures have, I believe, had minimal influence on how medicine is practised. The GMC might have managed to remove some of the grossest rogues from the profession, but how much influence has it had on the day-to-day practice of medicine?

Doctors might regulate themselves better if they acknowledged more the power of culture, colleagues and training. They might then introduce more formal appraisal and mentoring systems and do a better job of organising the training of young doctors. These things are beginning to happen – for instance, with the Calman proposals on specialist training. Doctors perhaps also need to do better with discouraging bad role models. Just as leading doctors who sets high standards of behaviour will have a profound influence so will those who behave badly. If junior doctors see senior doctors being short with patients, ageist and racist, sloppy in their research and haphazard in their time-keeping, then they are likely to behave in the same way. If they learn that the norm is to turn a blind eye to these behaviours – as it is – then they will too. This is one of the consequences of a culture of non-criticism.

Clinical experience

Clinical experience sounds like a good thing. Everybody would rather be treated by a clinically experienced doctor rather than by an inexperienced one. Does that mean, then, that older doctors are always better than younger ones? Age may or may not bring wisdom but it certainly brings experience. People are much less sure that an old doctor is better than a young one. They worry that the older doctor may not be up to date or may have a manner that is unsympathetic to patients who want to take charge of their own illnesses and bodies.

Doctors themselves set high store by clinical experience. If the 'evidence' says one thing and 'clinical experience' another, then doctors follow clinical experience. They have been upset by the implication of 'evidence-based medicine' that clinical experience may have a strong negative side. Clinical experience has to be considered in any essay on the forces influencing how doctors practise, whether they get better or worse, but it is hard to define. It is a set of knowledge and skills, but it also has to do with 'doctoriness.' Doctors' doctors are those blessed with clinical experience, but Michael O'Donnell, medical wit and essayist, defines it as 'making the same mistakes with increasing confidence over an impressive number of years'.[5]

Medical education

The medical education that I received in the early 1970s probably was not much different from that received by medical students a hundred years before. The developments of science, the appearance of antibiotics and other effective therapeutic interventions and the start of the NHS might have changed the practice of medicine, but I am sceptical that they have changed medical education much.

The content was different, but the process – of didactic courses with large amounts of material but small intellectual content followed by a clinical apprenticeship – was much the same. Indeed, medical education remained much the same for the following 20 years. Only now does there begin to be a switch in undergraduate education from memorising a mountain of material to learning how to solve problems.

Medical education is still, however, less about what is taught in the curriculum and more a process of learning the ways and culture of medicine.[6] Education locks people into a way of thinking and behaving that has a much more powerful influence on the way they practise in later life than does any number of messages from the GMC or guidelines from the health authority.

The early postgraduate years – the years in the trenches of medicine – are probably the most potent years of all for determining how doctors behave. Junior doctors have been called 'the lost tribes.' They wander through medicine with poor training and minimal career guidance searching for a home. Sometimes they wander for years and never arrive anywhere.

Specialist training has been a little better supervised, but it too has been mostly about learning a set of skills and attitudes on the job while spending the evenings learning arcane and often irrelevant material to pass professional exams.

Continuing medical education (CME) seems to be a new discovery in Britain. The magic acronym is heard on the lips of the senior doctors in royal colleges, and an industry is arising. But nobody seems clear how best to organise CME or whether it is effective. Indeed, the best evidence suggests that most of it is not.[7] The norm is for most doctors steadily to slide down in their knowledge and skills from the point where they complete their professional training – usually at about 30.[7]

Those interested in regulating the medical profession better need to think hard about medical education – harder, I suggest, than they think about the structure and function of the GMC.

Doctors' families

Doctors' families have an influence in that they are part of medical culture. A sizeable chunk – perhaps a third to a half – of British medical students are the sons and daughters of doctors. They are born into the culture. But the conjugal families of doctors also have an influence on doctors' behaviour – partly because many doctors are married to other doctors or to nurses or other health workers. Families also have an influence because they are insisting on more attention from doctors. One of the great divides in the recent intraprofessional debate over core values was on the importance of families. Older doctors tell stories – almost proudly – of never seeing their children growing up and insist that patients must come first. Younger doctors argue that it is highly abnormal to put patients before one's family and that patients will suffer if cared for by doctors who are so dysfunctional as to do so.

Pharmaceutical industry

The pharmaceutical industry may not have the power to strike a doctor from the medical register but it has powerful techniques at its disposal for influencing how doctors practise. It has far more information on doctors than does the GMC. It is concerned with the whole profession not just miscreants. And it has vastly greater resources than the GMC which it can use on 'education' and ever more sophisticated marketing. The industry may occasionally fall into disrepute for the extravagance of its junketing for ordinary doctors, but its marketing efforts are concentrated much more on strategies such as influencing opinion leaders through supporting their research programmes, paying for their registrars and secretaries, flying them (in business class at least) to conferences, and paying them handsomely for consultancies.

This activity rarely strays into the illegal, and the industry is doing the job it is required to do to satisfy its shareholders. But it is having a powerful influence on how medicine is practised – in every country.

Medical evidence

One of the myths of medicine has been that the practice of doctors has been driven in large part by science. Doctors, particularly those in general practice, have long been aware that much of what they do is far from 'scientific,' but the past five years have seen increased understanding of just how little of what doctors do is based on good evidence. This is partly because the evidence does not exist, partly because it is hopelessly disorganised, partly because doctors do not know about the evidence, and partly because there is a substantial gap between knowing about the evidence and applying it in practice. I have watched the phrase 'evidence-based medicine' go from something that led to blank looks in 1994 to something that is used in most medical conversations in 1997. Along the way it has created a considerable backlash – partly because doctors are afraid that its ideas will in some way be used to regulate what they do.

Various governments, including the British, have become very interested in evidence-based medicine. The British has tried various measures to encourage doctors to base their practice more firmly on evidence but stopped well short of compulsion. The French Government, in contrast, has tried to use the law to encourage more evidence-based practice.

Patients

The power of patients to influence medicine is undoubtedly increasing. The rhetoric of medicine has always been that the patient comes first, but it has not felt like that to many patients. They often feel that the primary function of the NHS is to satisfy the needs of health professionals, particularly doctors.

But patients are striking back. Within the consulting room relationships are beginning to change. AIDS patients have led the way, often knowing more about their condition than the doctors who are treating them and being fully aware of their rights and entitlements. Most doctors in Britain now have had the experience of a patient arriving with a collection of printouts from the world wide web. Some doctors resent this change but many are happy with this evolution from 'patients' to 'partners'.

Patients are also exercising greater power on the broader stage. Amateurish patient organisations are being replaced by much more sophisticated groups, usually organised around particular diseases. They employ high-powered chief executives on high salaries who use many of the techniques of the best run businesses. These new organisations may be much more effective at shifting the balance of power. Perhaps, for instance, the GMC will need to do more than simply increase the lay proportion of the Council – perhaps patients will eventually have to have a majority.

Medical press

Once a month I meet somebody who says to me, 'As the editor of the BMJ you must be one of the most influential figures in medicine.' I always demur. I answer – honestly – that it is hard to judge the influence of the BMJ or the rest of the press. Rarely does immediate action of any kind follow what is published in the medical press, and most research shows that medical journals have little direct influence on medical practice. The role of the medical press seems to be more to do with setting the agenda rather than deciding the outcome. And the medical press does not work through investigation and exposure. It has neither the resources nor the cultural inclination to do so.

Informal external forms of regulation

NHS managers

Ten years ago, NHS managers were called administrators by doctors and largely ignored. They set budgets and became involved if the behaviour of a doctor became so outrageous that it was bordering on the criminal or insane. The power of managers over day-to-day clinical practice was small and remains small. The managers of the NHS do not manage the main part of the business, the treatment of patients. It is as if the managers of McDonald's had no say in the food served in their restaurants. This may change, particularly as more and more managers are doctors and through the activities of managed care.

But even if the power of managers over doctors tends to stop short of directing their clinical activity, it is growing. Managers are steadily more involved in the hiring, training, rewarding and firing of doctors, and they have much greater influence in the running of the hospital or trust. Public health doctors are increasingly 'on tap rather than on top,' and hospital doctors may follow. General practitioners may think that they can resist managerial pressure because they have had their independent contractor status, but now salaried general practitioners are arriving. Perhaps the independent practitioners will go the way of the high street lawyer or butcher, beaten out of business by the large chains.

It seems inevitable that the power of NHS managers to regulate the work of doctors will grow. Perhaps there will come a day – maybe not so far away – when their 'regulatory' power will be greater than that of senior doctors.

Interaction between public officials and professional leaders

I picked up the regulatory influence of 'interaction between public officials and professional leaders' from the analysis of Allsop and Mulcahy,[1] but I am unconvinced that it counts for much. It is said that the Conservative Government spelt out to Robert Kilpatrick, the immediate past President of the GMC, that the Council would have to do something about those doctors whose performance was poor but who had not done anything bad enough to be deemed 'serious professional misconduct' (which is necessary if the Council is to remove a doctor from the register). The Council did under the leadership of Kilpatrick – and after years of procrastination – begin the process of constructing the machinery to deal with such doctors. This was introduced in the autumn of 1997.

It was inevitable that the Council would have to do something about doctors who consistently performed poorly. Pressure had come from within the Council, from the profession, from patients' organisations, from the media and from members of Parliament. If doctors were to continue to regulate themselves, then they had to act. Any mutterings from Government to the President of the GMC in the Reform Club were icing on the cake.

There is a steady stream of professional leaders travelling to Whitehall, but it is doubtful that this interaction has much influence on what is happening in the wards and surgeries – not least because doctors are unattracted by the notion of leadership.

General media

The general media strike fear into many doctors (and dreams of what Freud called 'fame and the love of beautiful women' into some others), but do they have much influence on how doctors practise? Doctors know the rush of patients after some scare stories: for example, the number of abortions and births both rose because of the pill scare of the autumn of 1995. The media may 'promote' diseases like myalgic encephalomyelitis, while ignoring the huge number of deaths from stroke and road traffic accidents. They may also investigate some rogue doctors and protest about doctors who are put back on the register after being struck off. But I contend that doctors think little about the mass media as they go about their daily practice. The media have little effect on whether doctors work to improve their performance or allow it to deteriorate.

Formal external influences

Employment and other contracts

Legal contracts are probably a more powerful external formal influence on medical practice than the courts. They are much more pervasive. Changes in the contract that general practitioners hold with the NHS can affect powerfully the way that they practise and behave. Thus the revised contract of 1990 led to a considerable increase in the amount of health promotion activity and much greater attendance at postgraduate education activities. The employment contracts of hospital doctors have less effect on the content of the professional practice and behaviour. There have, however, been many rows around 'gagging clauses,' which doctors see as an attempt by trusts to shift their primary loyalty from patients to employers. The Government also proposed writing into consultant contracts a requirement for them to report on any colleague who was underperforming. Doctors resisted this on the grounds that the GMC already required them to do it. Not that they do.

The behaviour of doctors is also influenced by the contracts that purchasers hold with trusts. This gives purchasers only the broadest brush influence on how doctors practise. Attempts to influence the 'quality' of what is done are at the beginning. There is clearly scope for the Government and NHS managers to use contracts to 'regulate' the behaviour of doctors, but they are a blunt instrument.

The courts

Doctors sometimes appear in the criminal courts for the same reasons as members of any other group. They sometimes appear there as well because of criminal charges that arise from their professional activity: doctors have been charged with manslaughter after gross mistakes, such as killing patients by injecting into the spine drugs intended for the veins. Or doctors may be charged with murder or manslaughter after hastening a patient's death at the patient's request. These criminal trials for offences committed during medical practice are so rare that they are unlikely to have much influence on routine medical practice. This conclusion is supported by the fact that many doctors say that they have intentionally hastened the death of a patient, despite the intention making this illegal.

Doctors are much more likely to appear in the civil courts because of negligence, and we seem to have reached the stage now where a doctor must expect to be sued during a professional lifetime. Do the courts have then much influence on the practice of medicine? It is hard to find convincing evidence that they do. It is argued that intraoperative deaths because of anaesthetic failure disappeared in the USA because of court actions, but I find it hard to think of a similar case in Britain. Obstetricians will often argue that Caesarean section rates are so high because of legal fears, but the evidence is unconvincing. A great many other factors are at play, and Caesarean section rates seem to have risen worldwide – unrelated to the nature of the legal system.

Audit Commission

The Audit Commission assumed responsibility for auditing the NHS in 1991 and may well have had some influence on what doctors do. The Commission has concentrated on activities that have large costs and where there seems to be scope for change. They began, for instance, with day surgery and observed wide variation among hospitals in the proportions of patients who were treated as day cases. The Commission produced detailed advice on how hospitals could increase the amount of day surgery. Through its local network of auditors, the Commission was then able to monitor the extent of day surgery, and it has increased considerably in the past five years. This might have happened anyway, but many believe that the Audit Commission does have an influence on doctors' work. It does this through carefully picking activities open to change, giving guidance for change, and auditing what happens. It also involves influential doctors in its studies.

Health Service Commissioner

The Health Service Commissioner – or 'ombudsman' – for years had no powers to rule on clinical matters. Now he does. This opens the possibility that he may be able to have some influence on how doctors behave, but this is likely to be considerably less than the influence of either the courts or the GMC.

NHS complaints procedures

The concept from continuous quality improvement that 'all defects are treasures' because they provide opportunities for doing better is a foreign notion to most doctors. They feel personally injured by complaints and have tended to resist and deny them rather than see them as opportunities for improvement. Perhaps as a consequence NHS complaints procedures are complex and unfriendly to patients.

Patients' organisations do not see the procedures as effective mechanisms for regulating the behaviour of doctors.

League tables

Governments are interested in the idea that league tables – ranking hospitals or even individual doctors by performance – may be a means of influencing the behaviour of doctors. The British Government has for some years published league tables of waiting times and other administrative measures, but it has been nervous about publishing tables of clinical measures such as death rates from heart attacks or postoperative infection rates. Such tables have now appeared in Scotland, however, and are promised for England.

There are many problems with such tables. The basic data may be lacking or inaccurate. Risk adjustment is difficult, meaning that some doctors or hospitals may seem to do 'badly' simply because they are treating sicker patients. Only some clinical activities are amenable to league tables, opening up the possibility of perverse incentives: managers and doctors may concentrate resources and energies on those activities that are measured – to the detriment of those many others that cannot be easily measured but may be more important.

These problems mean that league tables are unlikely to have much influence in improving doctors' performance.

Government/NHS

Most doctors in Britain work mostly within the NHS, and yet, I suggest, government ministers and the leaders of the NHS have limited impact on the performance of doctors. Doctors in the USA have resisted very strongly what they call 'socialised medicine' on the grounds that Government would influence their practice unduly. Ironically, most of those familiar with US and British practice would argue that lawyers, insurance companies, and now managed-care organisations, have much greater influence on the practice of US doctors than the Government has on the practice of British doctors.

Government ministers and NHS leaders are far removed from clinical practice. They have only blunt instruments for influencing the performance of doctors. They can use employment contracts, reorganisations of the NHS, exhortation, league tables and Executive Letters to try and influence doctors' performance, but these, I believe, have limited influence on how well doctors perform. They may have more influence on how much of different activities doctors undertake. For example, the Government may have used contracts with general practitioners to influence how much preventive work doctors did, but how could they influence the quality of that work?

Perhaps recognising their impotence, ministers and managers have been very interested in devices for influencing clinical practice – things like clinical guidelines and clinical audit. But the evidence suggests that the impact of these devices is small and happens only when doctors assume ownership. NHS leaders continue to search for mechanisms to influence the performance of doctors, and perhaps some of the many tools invented by managed-care organisations will help them.

Internal formal mechanisms

General Medical Council

An essay on the regulation of doctors in Britain might have begun and ended with the GMC with only limited mention of any other regulatory mechanism. But reading (particularly *Regulating medical work: formal and informal controls* by Judith Allsop and Linda Mulcahy)[1] and reflection have given me insight into the power of informal controls and the limited influence of formal mechanisms.

Self-regulation is important to doctors, but they have until recently taken it for granted. The current president of the Council, Sir Donald Irvine, does not, however.[8,9] He has reminded doctors that self-regulation is a privilege, not a right, and that they have to work hard to deserve it.[8] Doctors must be seen to be improving their performance.

The job of the GMC is to keep the register of doctors and through that ensure members of the public of the competence and professionalism of any registered doctor that they encounter. Logically, this means that the Council must have means for ensuring the competence and professionalism of those who are put on the register and for removing those who fall below minimum standards.

The Council began in 1858 and for many years was concerned primarily with sorting quacks from properly qualified doctors and arguing over who should be represented on the Council. It was decades before it developed mechanisms for dealing with wicked doctors. A penal cases committee was finally formed in 1893, and by 1915 most cases concerned doctors employing unqualified assistants and those canvassing, advertising, committing sexual misconduct, issuing false certificates, or performing abortions. Between 1919 and 1939 the committee heard only 311 cases – most to do with alcohol problems or false certification. Until recently, a common complaint against the GMC has been that it is very concerned with doctors who commit adultery with their patients but not much concerned with those who kill their patients through incompetence.

Various high-profile cases where doctors seemed to the public to have committed terrible offences but were not found guilty of serious professional misconduct by the GMC have forced the Council to develop mechanisms to do something about doctors who perform poorly but who would not be charged with serious professional misconduct. The need for such a mechanism was recognised by some members of the Council more than 20 years ago, but it began only in September 1997. The delay has been caused by several factors: the instinctive conservatism of doctors compounded by most of the members of the Council being senior and elderly; the Council's tradition of achieving consensus among the many factions of the medical profession, including the BMA, which represents the interests of doctors; the need to get parliamentary time to change the Medical Act, which governs the workings of the Council; and the need to establish and fund new machinery.

Will these mechanisms work and, even if they do, will they be enough to ensure the continuation of self-regulation? The mechanisms may not work because doctors continue to turn a blind eye to poorly performing colleagues. The system for detecting poorly performing doctors may prove inadequate. Then, it is likely to be difficult to rehabilitate doctors stuck in a pattern of poor performance that is derived from declining knowledge, falling skills, personality and psychological problems, and inflexible attitudes. And even if rehabilitation is possible, it may prove impossibly expensive. Managers running a cash-starved Health Service may find it much easier to sack or make redundant a poorly performing older doctor and replace him or her with a cheaper, more competent younger one. Or doctors at large may be unwilling to pick up the bill for retraining their poorly performing colleagues. Another problem might be that those doctors who find themselves about to have their right to practise removed are likely to use lawyers to fight their case, embroiling the Council in expensive and time-consuming legal battles. Cases appearing before the professional conduct committee are already tending to become longer.

There can be no doubt that the Council is committed to making this machinery work, and the president is anxious to increase the pace of reform within the Council and the profession. An early exponent of the value of continuous quality improvement within medicine, he wants to move the Council on from concentrating on what doctors should not do to being clear about what it means to be a good doctor. Although the Council will have to continue to respond to poorly performing doctors, he wants it to become much more concerned with maintaining and improving still further the performance of doctors who are doing well. 'To show that self-regulation is effective,' Sir Donald Irvine has written, 'we need to test the system against explicit criteria and standards, requiring hard evidence of compliance.'[8] One development is that the proportion of lay people on the Council will be increased to 25 per cent, and they will be involved in the teams assessing competence.

Sir Donald has explicitly acknowledged the threat to self-regulation.[8] Some argue, like George Bernard Shaw, that 'all professions are conspiracies against the laity.' Self-regulation of all groups – be it stockbrokers, members of Parliament, or the media – is increasingly suspect, with a falling proportion of people believing that professional standards are strong enough to resist the pressures to be self-serving and to close ranks. Free-market enthusiasts see bodies like the GMC as essentially anticompetitive devices designed to limit the number of people who can offer health care services and so keep up the price of services and the income of doctors. They would argue that the market would do a better job than the GMC of advancing those health care providers (be they doctors, nurses, osteopaths, or whoever) who perform well and removing those who do not. Others argue that the GMC should be replaced simply because it has not done well enough. It has taken almost a century and a half to develop a system for dealing with poorly performing doctors, has failed to find ways to develop sufficiently fast the education of doctors, and seems to have no effective system for dealing with problems like, for instance, research misconduct among doctors.

My bet is that self-regulation will survive because of the enormous political resources that would be needed to abolish it and because there is little evidence that any other system would be better. The work of doctors continues to be so complex that judgements on whether a doctor is doing well or badly will ultimately depend on the view of other doctors. Any state-sponsored body run by lay people would find itself heavily dependent on doctors. Such a body would also need to be funded by the state and would surely be much more costly to the state than the current body. My prejudice is to agree with Sir Donald that 'independence gives doctors that self-respect which motivates them to perform well' [8]. But even if heavily regulated by non-doctors I think that doctors would be adept at playing the system to put their own needs before those of the public. (I may seem to be contradicting myself here, but my Hobbesian view leads to me to the conclusion that 'if you treat people like animals, they will behave like animals' – with all apologies to animals who are generally much better behaved than people.)

Much more of a threat to the GMC's ability to improve medical practice than abolition is the strong culture of doctors that leads them to behave in certain ways whatever the protestations of the

GMC or its president. Sir Donald recognises this. 'Role modelling,' he writes, 'is a powerful force in medicine. Marinker used the term "the hidden curriculum" to describe the effect of professional attitudes and behaviour of clinical teachers on students and doctors in training.'[8] The Council could not abolish that hidden curriculum even if it wanted to, and it needs to recognise its own limitations in effecting reform. Members of the GMC, prominent members of the priesthood, probably do, but the public and critics may not.

Other formal medical bodies

Medicine contains many other formal bodies that claim an influence on how doctors behave and many informal and even secret bodies (dining clubs and the Masons) that also have a strong influence. Some of the royal colleges antedate the GMC by centuries and command strong tribal loyalty from their members and fellows. But their influence has been weakened by repeatedly splitting into specialist colleges, by the appearance of specialist associations (which grow up to be full colleges), and by their own inability to develop in a fast-changing world because of their often ancient, inflexible, centralised and highly elitist systems of governance.

The BMA, in contrast, may be restricted in its ability to develop because of its grass roots activists having too much influence. Over 80 per cent of British doctors belong, giving the association great strength – but this is weakened by often having to go at the speed of the slowest, which can be very slow.

Critics argue that medicine has far too many organised factions and so lacks central leadership and an ability to move fast. Such anxieties have led to attempts to reform an academy of medicine that might provide leadership. But existing bodies, anxious to preserve their influence, are likely to ensure that such an academy has a restricted role – perhaps within academic medicine.

These many bodies, particularly the royal colleges, do have a strong influence on how doctors practise day to day, but most have not been very effective at doing something about those who lapse into poor performance. That has been seen primarily as the job of the GMC, although the colleges, particularly the smaller ones, are usually 'very much closer to the action' than the GMC.

Conclusions

A great many forces influence the practice of doctors and help determine whether they improve their performance or allow it to deteriorate. Some of those forces have much greater influence than others because they are powerful and pervasive. Most powerful, I have argued, are informal internal forces, particularly medical culture and senior colleagues: the young doctor is much more influenced by the behaviour of senior colleagues than the fine words of the publications of the GMC. And medical culture – like all cultures – changes slowly, and that change cannot be easily managed.

I am not trying to argue that change does not happen and is impossible to achieve. All of these forces might be imagined as cascades of water – some the most desultory drip, others a waterfall – falling onto stones. Change does occur, but slowly, and it is not easy to direct that change. There are too many competing forces at work, with the most powerful being the hardest to control.

If I were the president of the GMC – the single figure most associated with regulation of doctors – then I would not despair. I would not allow myself to think that it would make little difference what I did but nor would I deceive myself about the strength of my powers. I would recognise that I had to play a long game, could expect only slow change and was limited in my power to direct that change. But I would hope that by understanding the multiplicity and complexity of those forces I would be better able to encourage doctors to improve their practice.

Note
Some sections of this paper overlap with material published in the BMJ[10] and in the preface to *Problem doctors*.[11]

References

1. Allsop J, Mulcahy L. *Regulating medical work: formal and informal controls*. Buckingham: Open University Press, 1996.
2. Bosk C. *Forgive and remember: managing medical failure*. Chicago: University of Chicago Press, 1979.
3. Smith R. Doctors and leadership. Oil and water? From: *Transactions and report of the Liverpool Medical Institution* 1992–93:34–44.
4. Rosenthal MM. Promise and reality: professional self-regulation and 'problem' colleagues. In: Lens P, van der Wal G (eds). *Problem doctors: a conspiracy of silence*. Amsterdam: IOS Press, 1997.
5. O'Donnell M. *A sceptic's medical dictionary*. London: BMJ Publishing Group, 1997.
6. Marinker M. Medical education and human values. *J R Coll Gen Pract* 1974; 24:83–94.
7. Davis DA, Thompson MA, Oxman AD, Haynes RB. Changing physician performance. A systematic review of the effects of continuing medical education strategies. *JAMA* 1995; 274:700–5.
8. Irvine D. The performance of doctors. I: Professionalism and self regulation in a changing world. *BMJ* 1997; 314:1540–2.
9. Irvine D. The performance of doctors. II: Maintaining good practice, protecting patients from poor performance. *BMJ* 1997; 314:1613–5.
10. Smith R. All doctors are problem doctors. *BMJ* 1997; 314:841–2.
11. Smith R. Preface. In: Lens P, van der Wal G (eds), *op. cit.*

Transforming London's health system

Autonomy and self-organisation in the swamp

David Towell
Fellow in Health Policy Development,
King's Fund Management College

R obert Maxwell is a man of many parts, as the breadth of contributions to this book implies. Robert joined the King's Fund, where I was already among the senior staff, in 1980. From my experience of working with him over the last 17 years, there are three main strands of his persona to which I want to draw attention – and which provide the inspiration for the essay which follows.

First there is London: more precisely the continuing struggle to improve the health and health care of London people and therefore the quality of the London health system. London is the largest and most diverse city in Europe. Health care is the most organisationally complex, politically sensitive and personally significant of its many public services. The mission of the King's Fund is to find practical ways of assisting London leaders and its people in addressing the tremendous challenges of achieving desirable change in this system. For over 20 years (prior to joining the Fund he was Secretary to the Special Trustees at St Thomas's Hospital), this agenda has been central to Robert's interests. Soon after arriving at the Fund, for example, he took personal responsibility for the Fund's London Committee and its programme of work (still continuing through the London Health Partnership) to improve urban primary care. He also initiated and served on the two independent Commissions on the future of services in the capital, the second of which has recently reported on *Transforming health in London*.[1]

Robert brings a great deal of wisdom to these challenges. He appreciates more than most that the 'problem' of London's health system is just as much about *how* informed change is to be achieved as it is about *what* future patterns of services will be required to meet changing needs. Two years after the first Commission's report, when the Government was still implementing the Tomlinson recommendations with gusto, Robert attracted some unpopularity in high places by writing a personal commentary, *What next for London's health care?*[2] This argues persuasively that while a long-term programme of reform remains essential, it is equally essential that this is pursued in ways which re-establish trust, promote openness and foster learning from experience as change proceeds.

This brings me to a second important attribute. The philosophy of 'Let a thousand flowers bloom' is usually attributed to Chairman Mao. In Robert's hands, I assume that Quakerism played a larger part in an approach to leadership grounded in the belief that if you bring people together and trust in their capacity for 'responsible creativity', then good things will happen. Certainly, at the King's Fund, Robert has relied heavily on trying to provide favourable conditions for a plurality of talents to engage productively with the Fund's mission and the opportunities offered by what is happening in the Fund's environment. More generally, he manifests a healthy scepticism about prevailing fads in policy-thinking or new technological fixes if too much is claimed for their ability to offer protection from the inherent uncertainties in anything so complex and conflict-ridden as future developments in health care. His preference instead is to put faith in the capacity of people to act with integrity and thoughtfulness in together building a different future and learning to live with the anxieties involved.

The third aspect of Robert's contribution I want to highlight complements the previous two. For many years, a regular answer to the question 'Where is Robert today?' has been 'In Court'. His service as a magistrate in South London is in part an expression of his commitment to the responsibilities of citizenship and in part a practical manifestation of an interest in justice, also represented, for example, in his celebrated paper on quality in health care.[3] More subtly, however, I think it also represents a belief in the importance, not least for the leader of an élite foundation with a mission for London, of keeping in direct touch with the everyday experience of 'ordinary' Londoners, particularly those suffering most from disadvantage. A Magistrate's Court offers constant reminders of Joan Baez's refrain that 'There but for fortune go you or I'.

This essay picks up the London focus and each of these themes to address the question of how the transformation of London's health system to meet the needs of Londoners into the 21st century might be achieved in the coming years. Of course the views which follow are mine, not necessarily Robert's. They are based on a series of empirical studies of recent experience of introducing change that my colleagues and I undertook for the second London Commission, published as London health care: rethinking development.[4]

My starting point is the questions of why significant change is needed in London and also why it is so difficult. Taking a lead from the themes outlined above, I then explore selectively the voluminous social science literature on large-scale change to identify a set of ideas which might be helpful to London leaders. The argument is that neither traditional conceptions of public sector planning nor the operation of market incentives fit well with the need for continuing evolution in both the organisation of health services delivery and forms of professional practice. Rather, progress depends on establishing a new culture and pattern of relationships in the health system as a whole which promote the *autonomy and self-organisation in the swamp* of the subtitle.

The swamp here is the complex and uncertain environment in which judgements about positive action must necessarily be made. Autonomy refers to the sense of individual authority (and therefore responsibility) required from a wide range of formal and informal leaders, to act on their own understanding of what is required to do better and learn from reflecting on this action as change proceeds. Self-organisation is the principle by which such autonomous leaders, confronted with the dilemmas of the swamp, work together often across existing boundaries, to establish more adaptive ways of organising and delivering responsive services to people and communities. Weaving these ideas together, it is possible to outline a new model for achieving transformational change and identify some of the conditions required for its application in London.

Unsurprisingly, there are significant cultural and political barriers to introducing these new ways of thinking and acting. If organisations are often memorials to old problems, conventional ways of thinking about organising provide the intellectual and emotional defence of these memorials. Writing in the summer of 1997, there is however a significant opportunity in London for reflecting on the experience of the past five years and discovering better ways forward. Both the new Government and, more specifically, its London Strategic Review open a window to different approaches to the next phase of health sector development. The essay concludes therefore with some implications for different types of leadership in London, including the future contribution of the King's Fund itself.

Addressing the London 'problem'

Across the developed world there are powerful pressures for change in health care systems, which make traditional patterns of services and the institutions providing them unstable. Most important are demographic changes, continuous innovation in treatment technologies and rising public expectations for high-quality services. New thinking about the shape of local services involves a fresh emphasis on primary care, pursuit of better co-ordinated support to enable people with chronic illnesses to sustain ordinary lives in the community and reshaping acute services to increase specialism and concentration in some, while others are delivered closer to home. There is also more explicit recognition of the growing inequalities in health in economically divided societies and of the need for priority-setting, as reasonable aspirations outpace the commitment to increasing public expenditure. At the same time the complexity of the interconnections between these pressures and their impacts makes prediction more than a few years into the future inherently risky. To quote Rudolf Klein, 'The only certainty is uncertainty.'[5] (p.8)

All this is of great importance to London as both the home for 7 million people and the UK's major centre for health services, education and research. Over the last century more than 20 separate inquiries have documented the need for significant change in the pattern of London services and institutions, largely with disappointing results.

In the 1990s, this reform agenda has focused on the three interrelated objectives of strengthening primary, community and continuing care; rationalising acute hospital services to improve quality and efficiency; and reorganising medical education and research into a small number of major academic centres. Although simply stated, the changes involved here are more profound than just the rearrangement of services and facilities: they imply a significant, medium-term *transformation* in which many people receiving care and many people providing it will be doing different things in different ways.

137

This agenda would be challenging anywhere but it is considerably more challenging in London. The size and diversity of London, its administrative complexity, the history of institutional parochialism and the tendency of local conflicts to be magnified by closeness to Westminster and the national media, all add to the difficulties for conventional approaches to securing planned change.

All major change programmes in public services pose difficult policy dilemmas, for example in balancing:

the Government's ultimate accountability and responsibility for fairness	*and*	the need for local discretion to ensure appropriate responses to diversity;
the authority of formal leaders to take action	*and*	the need to secure widespread commitment if this action is to be successful;
the requirement for conformity to agreed standards on some issues	*and*	the need for creativity to invent new 'solutions' on many others.

In the case of London's health system in the 1990s, three publications were particularly influential in shaping thinking on the response to these dilemmas: the report of the first London Commission,[6] the 'Tomlinson' report[7] and the Government's response to this, *Making London better*.[8] Each of these argues that change on the scale required in London needs a combination of clear strategic direction (e.g. 'strategic guidance ... and coherent system-wide implementation';[6] 'managed firmly'[7]) with some form of decentralisation (e.g. 'driven locally and, above all, by patient needs'[8]). However, the specific proposals in these reports leave unclear how these top-down and bottom-up elements are to be integrated. Indeed, the two official reports put all the emphasis on a traditional planning model relying on ministerial decision-making supported by a high-level implementation agency tackling major tasks on very short timescales.

The practice has turned out to be quite messy. The official approach to addressing the multiple London challenges has been based on what, at least initially, was a concerted package of top-down planning and promotional initiatives combining quite detailed prescription from the centre, active political leadership from the Secretary of State for Health, ear-marked funds both to promote innovation and cover the costs of transition, and new machinery for negotiating change across local and institutional boundaries (notably the short-lived London Implementation Group).

However, this London-focused package was being implemented alongside a wide range of other national policy initiatives aimed at both decentralising control in health and social services through introduction of the internal market, while retaining strong central prescription on all kinds of specific issues (e.g. the Calman reforms to medical staffing; the Culyer changes to R&D funding and, perhaps most significantly, the Private Finance Initiative on access to capital for investment).

Moreover, all this was only 'one side of the coin'. There were also the myriad initiatives taken by individuals and groups throughout the London health system on their own authority – sometimes responding to the official agenda, sometimes pursuing other goals – which were arguably just as much the real stuff of sustaining or changing existing arrangements.

At first sight, this combination of official measures and informal initiative suggests a potent mixture. Undoubtedly, a lot has happened over the last five years, as the second London Commission has sought to document.[1] The evidence collected by the Commission, however, also casts considerable doubt on the extent of progress in tackling the medium-term agenda required to serve Londoners better and the sustainability of some positive developments (particularly those designed to shift the balance between hospital and community services). It thus raises serious questions about whether these approaches to change are likely to be successful.

Perhaps with hindsight, we can see that while there is much to be commended in the high-level political commitment to reshaping

London institutions and the specific London policies, the ways change has been addressed also have major deficiencies.

While different types of change have different requirements, this mixture of centralisation and decentralisation, planning controls and market freedoms, has appeared poorly related to the real challenges. The scope for central planning and decision-making in change of this complexity was overrated. Health authorities and other agencies have been hard put to establish (let alone implement) a coherent local agenda in the face of a plethora of central policies and directives (some of which, like the private finance initiative, inhibited the changes that had been agreed).

At the same time, there has mostly been the wrong kind of decentralisation: market fragmentation and competition have been poorly equipped to handle politically and professionally sensitive changes over quite long timescales. In particular, the creation of NHS trusts as cost centres, often based on existing institutions, has added to the difficulties of securing a population-centred approach to service development across existing agency and professional boundaries.

Meanwhile the lip-service to philosophies which recognise the importance of both staff and public involvement in shaping and delivering change has often been difficult to realise, as decisions were taken 'behind closed doors', conflicts suppressed and public leaders turned into hostile bystanders. Change in management became the enemy of the management of change, as organisational turbulence undermined the continuity necessary to build confidence in the shift to new patterns of provision. All this and the intended pace of development have also meant that there have been inadequate arrangements for learning from experience across London as change has occurred.

Are there other ways of thinking about achieving strategic change in situations of this complexity which could assist London leaders in tackling better the massive agenda for development over the next five years? I think so.

Rethinking development

The popular dictum 'There is nothing so practical as a good theory' is usually ascribed to Kurt Lewin. It is certainly the case that if, as leaders and participants, we are to orient ourselves in complex and changing systems, we need the capacity for what Gareth Morgan describes as 'imaginization',[9] i.e. the use of theories and metaphors to find new ways of seeing, understanding and shaping our actions. Necessarily, all such metaphors are partial in the illumination they offer: in practice people need to be able to draw on a variety of perspectives which are themselves amended and extended through experience.

Social science, and in this case the extensive multidisciplinary literature on large scale change, provides for the systematic development of these theories, often drawing on the metaphors used by practitioners and in turn being selectively reincorporated into their repertoires. From this extensive literature, I want to introduce five interrelated sets of ideas (and their principal authors) which seem to have particular relevance to the London 'diagnosis' above.

Donald Schön: learning for action in a rapidly changing world

Nearly 20 years before the popularisation of ideas about *Thriving on chaos*,[10] Donald Schön set out a powerful critique of the failure of public agencies to adapt to the increasing rate of environmental change in *Beyond the stable state*.[11] Hierarchical forms of organisation and the separation of policy-making from implementation were no longer adequate to the challenges public agencies were established to tackle. Rather, Schön argues, organisations need to become *learning systems*, capable of bringing about their own continuous transformation through learning at the periphery of their activities and diffusing this learning through a wide variety of networks.

His subsequent work explores the implications of this view for the professional practice, for example, of policy-makers, managers and clinicians. In all these areas professional knowledge seems mismatched to what is increasingly required in everyday situations of complexity, uncertainty and conflicting values. Learning to cope with these conditions requires a shift in emphasis from the application of technical rationality (which can be taught) to the art of *reflection-in-action* (which can only be learned from experience). Schön writes:

> In the varied topography of professional practice, there is a high, hard ground where practitioners can make effective use of research-based theory and technique, and there is a swampy lowland where situations are confusing 'messes' incapable of technical solution. The difficulty is that the problems of the high ground ... are often relatively unimportant ... while in the swamp are the problems of greatest human concern. Shall the practitioner stay on the high, hard ground ... ? Or shall he descend to the swamp where he can engage the most important and challenging problems if he is willing to forsake technical rigour?[12] (p.42)

Henry Mintzberg: emergent strategy for public policy

Through a great variety of empirical studies of what happens in large organisations, Henry Mintzberg has developed these ideas with particular reference to *The rise and fall of strategic planning*.[13] He shows convincingly that the claims made for large-scale planning, not least in government, are largely unwarranted.

However, there is no need to throw out the strategy baby with the planning bath water. Defining strategy as the pattern that can be identified in many actions over time in a policy area, Mintzberg argues that it is useful to distinguish (as poles on a continuum) between two broad types of strategy: *deliberate* and *emergent*. Deliberate strategy is precisely the traditional conception of top-down planning, based on 'rational' analysis, which precedes implementation and becomes realised (or does not, as the case may be!). *Emergent strategies* by contrast can be recognised in what is achieved, but rather than being formulated in advance, emerge through a variety of processes characterised by flexible responses at the grass roots and the capacity within the organisation or system to learn from these responses in ways which give increasing shape to the patterns thus produced.[14]

What the empirical studies show is that in practice all policy-making involves a combination of deliberate and evolved action, in different mixes: for example, near the middle of the continuum are 'umbrella strategies' in which the 'top' provides guidelines or boundaries for local action, initiative is encouraged and patterns emerge within these boundaries which are carefully monitored.

Moving from description to prescription, the significance of these distinctions is to suggest that different types of change are likely to unfold in different ways under different conditions: in seeking to promote change therefore it is important to choose 'horses for courses'. Deliberate strategies are likely to be appropriate where the environment is stable, information for planning can be assembled centrally, 'solutions' can be standardised and people at the delivery end can be expected at least to acquiesce. Mainly emergent strategies, however, are appropriate in complex and unpredictable circumstances, where the required intelligence is located deep inside the system and action is dependent on motivated local leadership.

Margaret Wheatley: self-organisation to produce order out of chaos

The idea of emergence has been further developed by Margaret Wheatley among others, from a very different intellectual basis.[15] She points out that much organisational thinking is still grounded in a mechanistic and deterministic Newtonian view of the world. If we must look to natural sciences for metaphors, she argues that there is much more to learn from 20th century sciences such as quantum physics, chemistry and chaos theory, which offer a quite different view – of the need to look at the whole rather than the parts of natural systems, to appreciate the inherent uncertainty and unpredictability in much of the natural world and to see *self-organising systems* at work. Translating these ideas into organisational life she writes:

> What leaders are called upon to do in a chaotic world is to shape their organisations through concepts, not through elaborate rules or structures.[15] (p.133)

Ralph Stacey[16] has applied these ideas to the challenges of achieving large-scale change. He argues that organisational success requires the simultaneous practice of 'ordinary' and 'extraordinary management'. The former refers to the day-to-day management of existing services and their incremental improvement (very important, for example, in maintaining quality in public services). *Extraordinary management* by contrast is required to discover and implement radically new ways of doing things (i.e. to bring about the transformation of existing services).

Metaphors from the new sciences suggest that such transformations can be understood as seeking *order emerging from chaos*[17] through allowing but containing instability in existing arrangements, fostering informal self-organising networks and new alliances across agency boundaries, mobilising diverse perspectives (not just 'the usual suspects') and encouraging the active search for innovation.

John O'Brien: starting from individual experience

In human services it is of course essential that strategic change and service development are informed by, and ultimately tested against, the experience of people using these services. Writing about the last weeks of my father's life, I have myself documented the complexity and sensitivity of the professional and community action involved in this most common and unique of human experiences.[18] Working mainly on the challenge of how people with serious disabilities can get the opportunities and support to lead a rich life in the community, John O'Brien has illuminated the nature of the leadership required 'close to the ground' in tailoring support to individual needs.

He suggests that leadership entails encouraging attention to responsible visions of desirable futures for people and working to clarify the values which underpin these aspirations, discovering ways of working which enable staff to pursue these visions and relating outwards to generate the resources required to undertake this work. The focus on individuals further entails getting to know people using services well and creating small problem-solving networks, with and around the person, prepared to take action to move towards these better futures in the community. Most important, however, is the investment in learning which *embraces ignorance, error and fallibility.*[19] By showing the humility to listen to these 'three teachers' – ignorance about all that might be possible, error in working most effectively and fallibility in recognising the limits to professional services – organisations can become more competent in all these functions.

Eric Miller: *autonomy and negotiation in developing large systems*

Eric Miller has been the leading exponent of the distinctive Tavistock Institute approach to organisational change over more than 30 years. As the title of his overview of this work, *From dependency to autonomy,*[20] suggests, a central aim of this approach has been assisting people to gain greater influence over the things which affect them. A second key element has the been use of the biological analogy to examine individual and organisational life as 'open systems', i.e. as interrelated sets of activities or functions within some identifiable boundary which interact with each other and with the wider environment.

Autonomy at the individual level can be understood in terms of developing greater maturity in understanding and managing the boundary between the person's inner world (of values, intentions and anxieties) and the realities of the external environment. But the same ideas can be applied at larger system levels as, for example, in much of the early Tavistock work to establish autonomous work groups in industries like coal mining.

Miller has applied these ideas to change strategies in very large public systems, notably a massive programme of integrated rural development in Mexico. He argues that for development to become self-sustaining, the people in each local community had themselves to be committed to the programme:

> Each community needs to become a resilient system, capable of managing its own development both internally and in interaction with external systems.[21] (p.27)

In this context, neither 'top-down' (i.e. central planning) nor 'bottom-up' (i.e. entirely locally driven) methods of securing change are likely to be successful. Rather, Miller suggests a *negotiating model of central/local relationships* as a middle way, involving a direction-setting and regulatory role for the centre, an active development role for local communities, and a set of relationships between the two based primarily on negotiation and mutual adjustment. Thus this model offers a means of recognising legitimate national and political interests, while also promoting the collaboration and autonomy required to respond creatively to diverse local aspirations.

London implications

This has been only a brief detour into the relevant literature but our own empirical studies of change indicate that many of these insights are likely to resonate with the experience of London leaders seeking to learn from recent events. Moreover, as we have described in more detail elsewhere,[4] it is possible to weave these insights together to suggest a significantly different approach to transforming London's health system in the next five years. This has six main elements.

First, it will be important to draw from recent experience a better understanding of the nature of complex change in health systems and how different types of change unfold in different circumstances so as to tailor change initiatives to these different requirements. In particular, it will be necessary to distinguish changes which by their scale and sensitivity (e.g. reconfiguration of acute hospitals) require explicit political sanction from the many other service developments where there is greater local freedom; changes which are sufficiently definable in advance (e.g. the formula for fair resource allocation) to be planned centrally from all those whose complexity requires an 'umbrella strategy' with emergent local responses; and incremental changes (e.g. to improve standards in general practice) which can be delivered by ordinary management from more radical innovations (e.g. to shift the boundaries between hospital and community services) where 'extraordinary management' may be essential.

Second, Government will need to take the lead in developing a 'negotiating model' of central/local relationships sensitive to these different requirements – i.e. emphasising the role of the centre in setting broad directions for local interpretation, defining relevant parameters and promoting the conditions for local adaptability (notably, by moving away from the fragmentation of the internal market towards a new framework which fosters collaboration), while encouraging a more autonomous role for local agencies, wherever possible working in partnership.

Third, these partnerships will in turn be important in fostering new ways of working across existing organisational and professional boundaries to mobilise the creativity and diversity required to achieve transformation in the patterns of local services to meet changing needs (e.g. as proposed on a large scale in the 'Health Action Zones' or more modestly to improve the integration of services to particular 'client groups' such as older people with chronic illnesses).

Fourth, it will be necessary to strengthen the participation of the full range of local stakeholders in these change processes so that service developments gain the commitment and incorporate the 'hands-on' knowledge of those who deliver and receive services and are tailored to reflect cultural and other forms of local diversity.

Fifth, running through all these points is the need to develop and sustain more effective, locally rooted leadership, both formal and informal, capable of challenging old assumptions, articulating new visions, building support for different forms of practice and helping people 'work through' the anxieties always involved in significant change.

Finally, the next phase of health system development will require an enhanced commitment to learning from experience as change unfolds (e.g. through providing safe forums for reflection and mutual aid across agencies and localities) with a particular emphasis on making service development 'people centred', i.e. starting from individual experiences in constructing better ways of doing things and, conversely, testing more global propositions by their outcomes in the lives of intended beneficiaries.

This is, of course, no more than a sketch of a different way of thinking about achieving development. It is, however, part of the philosophy underpinning many of these insights that any new model of strategic change cannot be fully prescribed in advance but has instead to be created through the reflection, interaction and reflection-in-action of people with different responsibilities within the London health system.

Four broad sets of stakeholders seem particularly important here: ministers and their advisers, health sector managers, clinicians and local representatives of Londoners themselves. Each faces a different combination of opportunities and difficulties in shaping their future contributions.

The new Government has both the prime responsibility and the moral authority to renew the NHS through an emphasis on collaboration in delivering public health goals. Ministers need, however, to avoid the pitfalls of assuming, even with a huge parliamentary majority, that appropriate change can be delivered from the 'top' downwards or, given Labour's close identification with the NHS, of being too cautious to take the political risks associated with real innovation.

Managers, by virtue of their training and experience, should be most familiar with alternative ways of thinking about achieving change, but even so it would be a mistake to underestimate management investment in hierarchical control systems and implicit belief in the power of technical rationality to deliver 'solutions'.

Clinicians (i.e. medical, nursing and other 'front line' professionals) are likely to welcome greater recognition of their essential creative input to finding better ways of providing integrated, patient-centred services. However, they do not always show the same sophistication in understanding organisations as they do in appreciating the complexities of illness patterns and are sometimes predisposed to defend, rather than work across, existing boundaries.

Community representatives are similarly keen to be genuine partners in local dialogue but, after many years of doubtful influence, can easily be mobilised in the stance of 'the opposition which does not seek to govern'.

In the words of Sheryl Crow, 'No one said it would be easy'. The current 'window of opportunity' could, however, be used to establish greater confidence in the capacity of government and local leaders to work together to deliver positive change in London and thus establish a 'virtuous circle' of growing success. In turn, this would be one element in the larger task of (re)building a mature democracy fit for the 21st century.

There is also a very significant challenge here for the King's Fund itself – to match its distinctive contributions to policy analysis, action research and community development to priorities in the London change agenda and strengthen its role as the main node in a pan-London learning system designed to increase the capacity of London leaders to exercise *autonomy and self-organisation in the swamp*. As the King's Fund enters its second century of service to Londoners, success in this challenge would be a fitting tribute to Robert Maxwell's heritage.

Postscript. *Donald Schön, whose work is described here and who was a distinguished King's Fund International Visiting Fellow, sadly died while this book was in press. This essay is also offered as a very modest expression of appreciation for the inspiration he provided for so many of us.*

References

1. King's Fund London Commission. *Transforming health in London.* London: King's Fund, 1997.
2. Maxwell RJ. *What next for London's health care?* London: King's Fund, 1994.
3. Maxwell RJ. Quality assessment in health. *British Medical Journal* 1984; vol. 288, 12 May, 1470–2.
4. Towell D, Best G, Pashley S. *London health care: rethinking development,* London, King's Fund, 1997.
5. Klein R. *Coping with uncertainty in hard times: political and social factors in health futures.* London: King's Fund, 1996.
6. King's Fund London Commission. *London health care 2010: changing the future of services in the capital.* London: King's Fund, 1992.
7. Tomlinson B. *Report of the Inquiry into London's Health Service, Medical Education and Research.* London: HMSO, 1992.
8. Department of Health. *Making London better.* London, HMSO, 1993.
9. Morgan G. *Imaginization: the art of creative management.* London: Sage, 1993.
10. Peters T. *Thriving on chaos.* New York: Knopf, 1987.
11. Schön D. *Beyond the stable state.* London: Temple Smith, 1971.
12. Schön D. *The reflective practitioner.* London: Temple Smith, 1983.
13. Mintzberg H. *The rise and fall of strategic planning.* Hemel Hempstead: Prentice Hall, 1994.
14. Mintzberg H, Jorgensen J. Emergent strategy for public policy. *Canadian Public Administration* 1997; 30(2):214–19.
15. Wheatley M. *Leadership and the new science.* San Francisco: Berret-Koehler, 1992.
16. Stacey R. *Strategic management and organisational dynamics.* London: Pitman, 1993.
17. Stacey R. Strategy as order emerging from chaos. *Long Range Planning* 1993; 26(1):10–17.
18. Towell D. Revaluing the NHS: Empowering ourselves to shape a health care system fit for the 21st century. *Policy and Politics* 1996; 24(3)3:287–97
19. O'Brien J. Embracing ignorance, error and fallibility: competencies for leadership of effective services. In: Taylor SJ, Biklen D, Knoll J. *Community integration for people with severe disabilities.* London: Teachers College Press, 1987.
20. Miller EJ. *From dependency to autonomy.* London: Free Association, 1993.
21. Miller EJ. *Integrated rural development: a Mexican experiment.* London: Tavistock Institute, 1995 (First published in Spanish, 1976).

How helpful are international comparisons of health policy?

Ken Judge
Professor of Social Policy, PSSRU,
University of Kent at Canterbury

Scientific advance is very much an incremental process. Most of the time progress is made through small accretions of knowledge. Well-established propositions developed by one generation of scholars are subjected to detailed scrutiny by their successors, and new insights and theories flourish as a result. Such a process of development does not cast aspersions on the contributions of those at relatively early stages of the evolutionary cycle. Proposition, rebuttal and new theorising have a symbiotic relationship with each other. One generation of scholars very much depends on the contributions of earlier ones. Without them, there would be no advance. Given this commonplace state of affairs, especially in the natural sciences, it is surprising to encounter in the social sciences a certain degree of hostility to any attempt at questioning what appear to be well-established precepts. Nowhere is this more true than in comparative studies of health policy and health care systems.

Rudolf Klein suggests that one reason for this is that so many comparative analyses are driven by the domestic political values of the analyst concerned and guided by the availability of data rather than scientific or policy questions.[1] Whatever the reason, comparative studies do seem to generate more than their fair share of defensive posturing, and scholars often seem unduly reluctant to accept legitimate challenges to the validity of many cherished propositions. This is a particularly unfortunate state of affairs because comparative studies are difficult to do, and there are few analysts who labour in this territory who do not have a valuable contribution to make. But circumstances change, new data become available, old theories are supplanted or modified, and more sophisticated methods continue their inexorable march.

In his long period of involvement in health studies Robert Maxwell has made many distinguished contributions to comparative analyses, but he has always had the wisdom to recognise the tentative and fragile nature of many of his findings and cautioned that 'studies of this type are fraught with difficulties'. For example, in his widely quoted study of *Health and wealth: an international study of health-care spending* he details the many:

> problems of data availability and reliability ... One is forced to piece together from various sources information that has already been recorded for other purposes ... This involves facing major questions of comparability and therefore of definition.[2] (p.17)

However, despite these qualifications, Maxwell continues:

> international comparisons in the developed world [show] ... that
> the similarities among developed countries in health needs and the
> problems of trying to meet them are far more important than the
> differences ... Matters on which international comparisons are of
> special relevance ... [include] whether we are expecting too much
> of the NHS for what we put into it (i.e. whether it is underfinanced
> relative to the level and scope of services aimed for).[2] (p.18)

I share the view that comparative studies do have a valuable
contribution to make to challenging and enhancing policy imagination,
provided that the cautionary notes of those such as Robert Maxwell
are always borne in mind. To illustrate the need for continued
vigilance in this area, I want to discuss some seemingly plausible
and well-established views about health policy which have found
themselves under critical review in recent years. The three
propositions are:

- variations in aggregate levels of health care spending are primarily
  a function of national prosperity;
- the distribution of income in advanced industrial societies is the
  primary determinant of variations in average levels of population
  health;
- more liberal and generous welfare states such as Sweden generate
  fewer inequalities in health status among their citizens than do
  more parsimonious Anglo-Saxon ones such as the UK.

National prosperity and health care spending

Health-care spending is very closely related to the means available.
The higher a nation's GNP, the higher tends to be the proportion
of that GNP related to health care.[2] (p. 102)

One of the most well-established findings in studies of comparative
health systems is that richer countries spend relatively more on their
health care systems than do poorer ones. For more than 30 years a
steady stream of research studies by some of the most influential
health policy analysts on both sides of the Atlantic, such as Joe

Newhouse[3] and Tony Culyer,[4] and including a distinguished contribution by Robert Maxwell,[2] has told a largely consistent story. First, that national prosperity, conventionally measured by GDP per capita, is far and away the most important determinant of observed variations in health care spending. Second, that as countries become richer they allocate a greater share of their national income to health care. Over the years, this literature has become ever more sophisticated but the broad conclusions remain the same.

> The use of different empirical models in analysing health expenditures in both OECD and developing countries has been quite diverse. While the early literature focused on the simple relationship between income and health spending, subsequent research efforts attempted a more in-depth analysis of the determinants of health expenditures by incorporating additional variables in the models and by using different techniques (including cross-section, time-series and pooled cross-section analysis), with varying degrees of success. Much consideration has also been given to methodology and the appropriateness of the technique(s) implemented. As cross-section (and latterly pooled cross-section) analysis dominated the empirical literature, one of the most important issues was the use of a conversion method, whereby economic data from each country were expressed in a common currency. The debate here focused on the use of exchange rates, purchasing power parities (PPPs) and average wage earning power. Regardless of the methodology and the type of model, the key results remain the same over time.[5] (p.4)

Despite the well-entrenched nature of the proposition that 'the wealthier a country is, the higher tends to be the proportion of its wealth spent on health care'[2] (p.100), a study from LSE Health challenges the validity of this claim. Kanavos and Mossialos[5] claim that insufficient attention has been paid to both theoretical and methodological considerations and argue that: 'The relationship between GDP and health care expenditure in a country is weak and ambiguous, and, consequently, its use over the past thirty years may have largely been exaggerated' (p. viii). Some of the reasons that they advance for questioning the association of GDP with health spending include substantial international variations in the definition and measurement of such phenomena as:

- estimates of GDP per capita
- the coverage of health care spending
- the size of the informal sector
- the impact of demographic change
- the diffusion of medical technologies
- the public-private mix of health care provision.

Some of these factors can be illustrated relatively easily. One of the most important is the need for a consistent definition of health care spending. At present there is considerable variation between countries in relation to spending on long-term care for elderly people, R&D and medical education. Spending on such items can be either totally or partially excluded in some countries and included in others. The picture can be further complicated by the fact that substantial chunks of health-related spending can be added to or removed from the formal health care budget by administrative strokes of the pen. This can encourage quite misleading inferences about trends in particular countries.

For instance, Sweden's health reform policies in the 1990s were considered to be successful in containing costs (in fact reducing costs) because health spending as share of GDP fell from nearly 9% to 7.3% of GDP. However, this was largely due to the shift of costs on long-term care and home care from the health budget to the social security budget (due to a devolution of power from the county councils to the municipalities).[5] (p.11)

One indicator of the extent to which definitional and compositional differences in health care spending vary can be illustrated by comparing the proportion of total spending consumed by hospital in-patient care. The OECD data bank shows that the proportion ranges from less than one-third in Germany and Japan to almost three-fifths in Denmark and New Zealand.

However, the problems are not confined to spending on health care. The consistency of estimates of national prosperity also varies considerably between countries. The European Commission has expressed considerable reservations about the methods employed in a number of countries, and this has resulted in considerable changes in the size of GNP in many countries. For example, in 1991, estimates were increased by between 15 and 20 per cent in countries such as Greece and Portugal. In richer countries such as Italy and Sweden there are thought to be major and unresolved problems in taking account of economic activities in the informal or parallel sector.

The main point of these and related arguments is to claim that the observed relationship between GDP and health spending is unhelpful and almost certainly misleading. It can have the effect of reducing domestic political debate about the adequacy of health spending within any particular country to a banal level. It deflects attention away from more informative analyses that would focus attention on the determinants of variations in the coverage and composition of health services. The conventional approach also fails to pay sufficient attention to the impact that health-related behaviours – such as smoking and diet, demographic change and the diffusion of new technologies might be expected to have on demands for additional spending. If the next generation of comparative studies of health spending focused more attention on these kinds of questions, they would make a much more useful contribution to practical health policy development than the continuous recycling of the putative association between prosperity and spending which may turn out to be an artefact of measurement error.

Income inequality and population health

[I]nequality per se is bad for national health, whatever the absolute material standards of living within a country.[6]

From both a historical and global perspective it is a relatively simple matter to demonstrate that economic and social development is the primary influence on population health. For example, there appears to be a strong association between GDP per capita and average life expectancy at birth when all nations are considered together, but this relationship is much less significant among the sub-group of richest nations.[7,8] As a result, there is a widely held belief that the influence of economic development on the health of a nation diminishes as prosperity increases.

In recent years a new body of argument has emerged which suggests that it is the shape of the distribution rather than the total size of national income available to rich countries that helps to account for observed variations in common indicators of population health such as life expectancy or infant mortality. For example, Quick and Wilkinson[9] have suggested that: 'Health differences between developed countries reflect, not differences in wealth, but differences in income distribution ... this seems to be the single most important determinant of why health in one country is better than in another.'

There are good grounds for believing that the existence of a link between income inequality and average levels of population health is a plausible proposition. Why should this be so? At its most straightforward the answer is a matter of simple mathematics, given the existence of a non-linear relationship between income and health at the individual level.[10] The gradient is steepest among low income groups, which means that any unit change in income should result in a bigger change in health among lower than higher income groups. It follows that:

> at the same national income, a more equitable distribution of income among households would be expected to produce a higher average life expectancy than countries with income maldistributed.[11] (p.149)

During the past 20 years or so a number of studies have been published that provide empirical support for the claim that various measures of income inequality are significantly associated with a range of indicators of population health such as life expectancy and infant mortality. The difficulty is that many of these studies are flawed by methodological problems. The most serious of these is that the income distribution data used by most of them leave much to be desired and in other cases insufficient attention has been paid to the way in which available data are utilised for analytical purposes. Two examples of the kinds of problems that can arise are set out below.

One of the most cited studies in recent years by Rogers[12] used data provided by Paukert[13] to investigate the relationship between income distribution and mortality *circa* 1965. However, the data obtained by Paukert actually range from 1948 (Italy) and 1957 (Israel) to 1969 (USA). It is doubtful whether such differences can reasonably reflect the relative degree of income inequality that existed between countries in the mid-1960s on a consistent basis. Moreover, the data are not adjusted for tax and benefits or household characteristics. In fact, Paukert himself is so cautious about the income distribution data that he has identified that he reproduces a passage from Simon Kuznets to make the point that:

> it may not be an exaggeration to say that we deal here not with **data** on the distribution of income by size but with estimates or judgements by courageous and ingenious scholars relating to the ... distribution of income in the country of their concern.[13] (p.113)

Probably the most well-known work is associated with Richard Wilkinson.[14] However, Judge[15] and Saunders[16] have both criticised his findings on a number of grounds. Judge shows that two of Wilkinson's most frequently reported analyses are flawed by errors in the computation and the selection of measures of income distribution. When these mistakes are corrected, the very substantial correlation coefficients between income distribution and life expectancy reported by Wilkinson are replaced by very much smaller ones that cease to be significant. Saunders argues, in particular, that Wilkinson's use of poor data for Germany and Switzerland had the effect of exaggerating the income inequality–health relationship. Using new data for these two countries, Saunders replicated Wilkinson's analysis but found that the relationship between income distribution and life expectancy disappeared. Saunders argued that this:

> highlights the simplistic nature of the view that there is a single relationship between life expectancy and income distribution. At the very least, one would expect other variables to intervene in ways which would make any simple correlation unlikely, indeed implausible.[16](p.44)

Although most of the studies published to date report some significant associations between income inequality and population health, the methodological problems highlighted above, among others, cast doubt on the reliability of their results. Overall, it seems reasonable to agree with Le Grand, who concludes that:

> given the weaknesses of some of the data (particularly, those for income inequality), the small sample sizes, and perhaps most crucially, the absence of an underlying theoretical structure within which to interpret them, too much should not be made of these results.[17] (p.189)

The question that remains, if it is the case that there are good theoretical reasons for believing that there might be a relationship between income inequality and average levels of population health, is whether or not any significant empirical relationships can be established. Using the most authoritative data on the distribution of income published by the OECD and obtained from the Luxembourg Income Study (LIS), a recent paper by Judge et al.[18] sets out to investigate the nature and strength of the relationship.

Judge et al.[18] conducted a careful analysis of the relationship between some of the most commonly used indicators of income inequality – such as the Gini coefficient – and measures of population health – such as life expectancy and infant mortality – using data for 14 of the richest industrial nations. In contrast to most previous studies, they find no support for the claim that income inequality is statistically significantly associated with life expectancy at birth. It is most certainly not the most important determinant as some studies claim. There is some suggestion that income inequality might be associated with infant mortality but the relationship is not a very strong one and it is complicated by the fact that the USA is such an extreme outlier in terms of its very high level of income inequality and its poor record of infant mortality.

Why are these findings so much at odds with most previous studies? One possibility is the phenomenon of 'publication bias'. There is clear evidence that many researchers are inclined to look for positive and/or novel results in the belief that this will increase their chances of publication in peer review journals.[19]

A more significant explanation may be a consequence of improvements in the quality of income distribution data. Any attempt to compare income distributions across countries, or across time, raises many problems, but the work of the LIS has led to very substantial improvements in the quality and consistency of the estimates that are now available. There can be little room for doubt that the estimates produced by Atkinson et al.[20] are the most authoritative and accessible to date.

Even so they are not perfect. As Atkinson et al.[20] acknowledge: 'The aim is to increase the degree of cross-national comparability, but *complete* cross-national comparability is not attainable. Comparability is a matter of degree, and all that one can hope for is to reach an acceptable level'. Nevertheless, it is clear that there is a very substantial difference in the quality of the income data between that used by, say, Rogers[12] and that reported by Atkinson et al.[20] in terms of both the consistency and the appropriateness of the measures used.

However, it is important to acknowledge that international comparisons of complex phenomena are notoriously problematical. It is clear that at the individual level low incomes are associated with poor health and that the overall shape of the income distribution might be expected to influence average levels of national health. But a nation's health is likely to be the product of a wide range of cultural, economic and social factors, many of which are not easily measured and most of which might interact with each other. What this implies is that one cannot state with confidence that income inequality is not associated with national health. With better data for more countries it might be possible to identify a significant statistical relationship. For the moment, all one can say is that the latest results based on the best data available provide only very modest support for the view that income inequality is associated with variations in average levels of national health among rich industrial nations.

In the context of WHO's commitment to encouraging a reduction in the variations between nations, this critique is not a particularly negative one because in recent decades there has been a considerable convergence in average levels of population health among the richest industrial nations. However, there has been much less progress in reducing inequalities in health between social groups within nations. Whether or not international comparisons can contribute to policy learning in this area is the next question to be addressed.

Welfare states and health inequalities

Cross-national comparisons of health inequalities are treacherous.[21] (p. 21)

Since the election of the Labour Government in May 1997, there has been an explosion of interest in health inequalities. New research or enquiry or commentary emerges almost every day. But there is a marked absence of any very compelling evidence about policies to tackle inequalities. Much of what passes for policy analysis in this area is largely either a litany of complaint about past injustices introduced or exacerbated by the Thatcher Governments in the 1980s or wistful glances in the direction of more liberal welfare states that are thought to have a better record in tackling health inequalities than Britain. Some support for the latter view can be found in one of the best known reviews of these issues, which concludes that:

> the comparative studies quoted lend support to the suggestion that the Nordic countries ... experience less social inequality in health than other European countries, including England and Wales.[22] (p. 310)

It now seems to be widely believed that Nordic countries such as Sweden have more egalitarian welfare states than countries such as Britain and that this accounts for their relatively low social variations in health. The question that I want to address is: does this proposition stand up to close scrutiny? To do this one needs to examine two further questions. Are there well-established and consistent differences between welfare states? Are variations in health inequalities associated with these differences?

There certainly seem to be well-established differences between welfare states among the richest OECD countries. A common feature of comparative social policy has been the classification of types of welfare state, and Esping-Anderson's[23] typology is perhaps the most well known. One of the most recent contributions to this literature distinguishes between countries on the basis of (a) the proportion of GDP allocated to social expenditure, and (b) whether or not the social welfare tradition in the country is best characterised as Bismarckian or Beveridgean, which in turn is measured by the extent to which social expenditure is financed by taxes or contributions.[24] The application of this classification to European welfare states is illustrated in Figure 1.

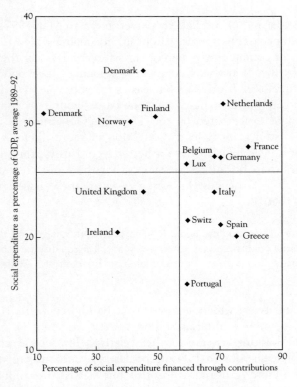

Figure 1 A classification of European welfare states
Source: Bonoli [24]

The most striking feature of ... Figure 1 is the correspondence between the four quadrants and the geographic position of the countries. The Nordic countries are in the top-left quadrant; continental European welfare states are in the top right-hand quadrant. Britain and Ireland are in the bottom left-hand quadrant; while southern European countries ... can be found in the bottom-right quadrant. This picture also reflects the most widely used classifications of welfare states.[24](p.360)

What seems clear then from this classification, and others similar to it, is that there are marked differences between welfare states and that countries such as Sweden are markedly more generous or liberal or egalitarian than Britain.

The Scandinavian model with an emphasis on universalistic and egalitarian social policies has been regarded as paradigmatic for a welfare state ... Britain illustrates a more 'liberal' societal development with a 'residual' social welfare model.[25](p.214)

Such variations create an incentive for comparative studies of health inequalities especially when, as now in Britain with the establishment of Sir Donald Acheson's inquiry, there is renewed governmental interest in the role that new public health policies can contribute to equity in health and health care. It is widely believed that domestic health policy can be informed by international comparisons.

Britain can learn from health trends and patterns in countries with similar and divergent socio-economic environments. These might provide clues both to causes of the observed patterns and to policy options for tackling inequalities in health (p.45)... Evidence from different countries and at different times within the same country of changing patterns of inequalities has provided encouragement that the health divide is not inevitable, but may be amenable to reduction by purposeful policy action.[26] (p.53)

Given that welfare states do appear to vary in what might be policy-relevant ways, is it possible to find evidence that health inequalities in Britain are greater than in social policy paragons such as Sweden? The early evidence appeared to suggest that this was the case. A much cited paper published in *The Lancet*[27] showed that class differences in mortality were substantially greater in Britain than in Sweden. The ratio of relative risks of mortality for social classes IV & V combined compared with I & II, was 1.48 in Britain in 1970–72 compared with 1.27 in Sweden in 1961–79. The authors concluded that:

> for 50 years Swedish governments have had a consistent commitment to the eradication of class inequalities, and educational, social, and health policies have been designed accordingly ... the less striking health differences between social classes in Sweden may indicate that consistent attempts to reduce class inequalities through general welfare policies have had an effect. (p.36)

Evidence such as this encouraged commentators to be optimistic about the role of international comparisons in supporting the case for more egalitarian social policies to tackle health inequalities. For example, in a review article in the *British Medical Journal*, Power noted that:

> the universal pattern of social differences in health in European countries is striking, but the variations between countries shown here ... suggest that such differences are not immutable. Sweden and Norway are particularly notable, with relatively low social differentials in both mortality and morbidity (p.1156) ... It is particularly notable that mortality differentials are smallest in countries with well-established social policies to improve the living conditions of the most disadvantaged sections of the population.[28] (p.1155)

Unfortunately for this mode of thinking, more recent evidence has questioned whether or not the differences in health inequalities between Britain and Sweden are as striking as was first imagined. For example, in a comparative study of social class differences in infant mortality between Britain and Sweden, Leon *et al.*[29] report that inequalities in post-neonatal mortality were of 'roughly the same magnitude' in both countries. Similarly, in their analysis of self-reported morbidity in Britain compared with Finland, Norway and Sweden, Lahelma and Arber report that, contrary to their expectations, health inequalities are more and not less pronounced in the Nordic countries.

> The finding that both for men and for women in Britain the degree of class differentials in illness is smaller than in the Nordic countries was not expected given that ... the Nordic countries represent 'social democratic welfare states, which follow a more egalitarian welfare model than the British 'liberal/residual' welfare state. On the basis of the typology of welfare states we could not predict the observed differences in the degree of health inequalities between Britain and the three Nordic countries.[25](p.224)

However, these authors do acknowledge the many difficulties associated with comparative research of this kind. For example, there are many international differences in social structures and cultures and because these may affect respondents' reports of ill health in the different countries, the available data may not yield robust indicators of health inequalities for comparative purposes.

But the sceptical cat has been most obviously set among the egalitarian pigeons with the publication of probably the most authoritative and comprehensive comparative study of health inequalities in Europe undertaken so far. An EU-sponsored concerted action[21] led by Johan Mackenbach, an internationally respected epidemiologist from Erasmus University in The Netherlands, has attempted to provide an overview of the international pattern of socio-economic inequalities in morbidity and mortality. A key finding for present purposes is that:

> socioeconomic inequalities in morbidity or mortality were not found to be smaller in countries with more egalitarian socioeconomic, health care or other policies. The magnitude of health inequalities in different European countries seems to be determined in part by circumstances that are not yet well understood.[21] (p.4)

This conclusion is of such potential significance for health policy development that it merits closer scrutiny, and one way of doing this is to examine the results obtained for Britain and Sweden in a little more detail. The key findings are shown in Table 1.

Table 1 Health inequalities in Britain

COUNTRY	MORBIDITY 25-69 [1]					MALE OCCUPATIONAL MORTALITY [2]			
	MEN			WOMEN		30-44		45-59	
	Education	Income	Occupation[2]	Education	Income	with*	without*	with*	without*
(1)	(2)	(3)	(4)	(5)	(6)	(7)	(8)	(9)	(10)
Sweden	4.84	3.12	16.1	7.27	3.73	14.5	12.3	10.2	7.3
Great Britain	4.06	4.62	10.9	4.02	4.39				
England & Wales						12.6	11.7	9.3	8.4

Notes
1. Relative index of inequality
2. Index of dissimilarity
* with or without adjustment for people who are economically inactive

Source: Kunst et. al.[21] Tables 8a, 8b, 10a, 10b, 11, 19

Columns 2–6 of Table 1 summarise the information obtained by the EU concerted action in terms of morbidity among men and women aged 25–69. Columns 7–10 show data for male mortality for ages 30–44 and 45–59 with and without adjustment for people who are economically inactive. The statistics shown are the relative index of inequality and the index of dissimilarity, and in each case the larger the number, the greater is the degree of inequality. Six of the nine pairwise comparisons illustrated imply that health inequalities are greater in Sweden than in Britain or England and Wales.

However, there are a number of methodological issues that have to be borne in mind in interpreting the data. First, it should be noted that the choice of numerator has an important bearing on the morbidity results. If social groups are segregated by education or occupation, then Sweden appears to be worse than Britain; however, if income is used, then the opposite is the case. Second, the subjective health indicator used as a proxy for morbidity differs between the two countries, and the absolute proportions of people reporting not good health in Sweden are substantially lower than in Britain. There are also problems with the interpretation of the mortality data because previous occupational information for men currently classified as economically inactive is unavailable, and such men have high death rates. Simply excluding such men from the analysis underestimates, and in some cases biases, the size of inequality estimates. The project team therefore developed a formula to adjust for this problem. Columns 7 and 9 show greater differences in health inequalities between Britain and Sweden when these adjustments are made than when they are not (columns 8 and 10) However, the confidence intervals around the adjusted estimates are wider for Sweden than for Britain.

What this all means in brief is that Anglo-Swedish comparisons of health inequalities are much more complex than previously thought. What this implies is that while it might not be safe to say that Sweden is worse than Britain, as the results might suggest at first sight, there appears to be no basis for thinking the opposite. It is certainly the case that the richness and variety of the evidence now becoming available has encouraged some enthusiasts for international comparative studies to be more circumspect than they might once have been.

> In recent years there have been increasing efforts to compare the level and nature of social differentials in health in different countries more directly. While valuable information could be gained from such comparisons, there are particular methodological problems which make the task highly complex and fraught with potential pitfalls.[26] (p.61)

It is difficult to argue with this conclusion. Students of comparative health should proceed with extreme caution. Nevertheless, it is important not to lose sight of the fact that the latest evidence does not support the conventional view that Sweden's more generous welfare state has yielded a better return in tackling health inequalities than has Britain's more parsimonious one.

Conclusion

> [T]here are all kinds of pitfalls in international comparisons. Nevertheless, some valid conclusions can be drawn, particularly about the many striking similarities among countries. Differences must be treated with more caution, as pointers to questions, rather than as answers.[30] (p.7)

No matter what question is being asked, or whatever the data that are being used, comparative studies are full of traps for the unwary. A healthy dose of scepticism and a willingness to expose statistical analysis to microscopic examination can be safely recommended for the budding analyst of international variations in health policy. But does this imply that comparative studies have little to offer and should be discouraged? That is not my view, and I am sure that such a proposition would not meet with Robert Maxwell's approval. There are many reasons why international comparisons of health care systems and population health characteristics are worth pursuing. It is certainly important to ask how one country compares with another in order for domestic policy-makers to try to form some judgement about the relative size or importance of the problem or issue they are considering. Descriptive studies can be very illuminating and often help to identify specific areas of interest for more detailed scrutiny. The main problem arises when comparative analyses are used for explanatory purposes. It is not that this is an illegitimate aspiration but that the data that are normally available do not lend themselves to sufficiently robust forms of analysis. If future attempts at international comparisons, and especially statistical ones, are to be more useful, then greater efforts will have to be made to organise special collections of data on a consistent basis across nations. In this respect it is important to applaud a recent initiative by The Commonwealth Fund of New York which is due to launch an annual international health policy symposium in 1998 based in part on new and more consistent data from many of the richest industrial countries.

References

1. Klein R. Risks and benefits of comparative studies: notes from another shore. *The Milbank Quarterly* 1991; 69(2):275–91.
2. Maxwell R. *Health and wealth: an international study of health-care spending.* Lexington: DC Heath, 1981.
3. Culyer A. Cost containment in Europe. *Health Care Financing Review* 1989; Annual Supplement: 21–32.
4. Newhouse JP, Cross national differences in health spending: what do they mean? *Journal of Health Economics* 1987; 6: 109–27.
5. Kanavos P, Mossialos E. *The methodology of international comparisons of health care expenditures: any lessons for health policy?* London: London School of Economics, (undated). Health Discussion Paper No. 3
6. Davey Smith G. Income inequality and mortality: why are they related? *BMJ* 1996; 312: 987–8.
7. Marsh C. *Exploring data: an introduction to data analysis for social scientists.* Cambridge: Polity Press, 1988.
8. World Bank. *World development report 1993: investing in health.* New York: Oxford University Press, 1993.
9. Quick A, Wilkinson RG. *Income and health.* London: The Socialist Health Association, 1991.
10. Backland E, Sorlie PD, Johnson NJ. The shape of the relationship between income and mortality in the United States: evidence from the national longitudinal study. *Annals of Epidemiology* 1996; 6:12–20.
11. Murray CJL, Chen LC. In search of contemporary theory for understanding mortality change. *Social Science and Medicine* 1996; 36:143–55.
12. Rodgers GB. Income and inequality as determinants of mortality: an international cross-section analysis. *Population Studies* 1979; 33:343–51.
13. Paukert F. Income distribution at different levels of development: a survey of the evidence. *International Labour Review* 1973; 108(2–3):97–125.

14. Wilkinson RG. *Unhealthy societies: the affliction of inequality*. London: Routledge, 1996.
15. Judge K. Income distribution and life expectancy: a critical appraisal. *BMJ* 1995; 311:1282–5.
16. Saunders P. *Poverty, income distribution and health: an Australian study*. Social Policy Research Centre Reports and Proceedings, 1996:128.
17. Le Grand J. Inequalities in health: some international comparisons. *European Economic Review* 1987; 31:182–91.
18. Judge K, Mulligan J, Benzeval M. Income inequality and population health. *Social Science and Medicine*. In press.
19. Easterbrook PJ, Berlin JA, Gopalan R, Matthews DR. Publication bias in clinical research. *The Lancet* 1991; 337:867–72.
20. Atkinson AB, Rainwater L, Smeeding TM. *Income distribution in OECD countries*. Paris: OECD, 1995:18
21. Kunst AE, Cavelaars AJEM, Groenhof F, Geurts JJM, Mackenbach JP and the EU Working Group on Socioeconomic Inequalities in Health. *Socioeconomic inequalities in morbidity and mortality in Europe: a comparative study*. Main Report: 1. Rotterdam: Department of Public Health, Erasmus University, 1996.
22. Whitehead M. *The health divide*. Harmondsworth: Penguin, 1992.
23. Esping-Andersen G. *The three worlds of welfare capitalism*. Cambridge: Polity Press, 1990.
24. Bonoli G. Classifying welfare states: a two-dimension approach. *Journal of Social Policy* 1997; 26(3):351–72.
25. Lahelma E, Arber S. Health inequalities among men and women in contrasting welfare states: Britain and three Nordic countries compared. *European Journal of Public Health* 1994; 4(3):213–26
26. Whitehead M, Diderichsen F. International evidence on social differentials in health. In: Drever F, Whitehead M (eds). *Health inequalities: decennial supplement*. ONS series DS15. London: The Stationery Office, 1997: 44–68.
27. Vagero D, Lundberg O. Health inequalities in Britain and Sweden. *The Lancet* 1989;35–6
28. Power C. *Health and social inequality in Europe* BMJ 1994; 308:1153–6
29. Leon DA, Vagero D, Otterblad Olausson P. Social class differences in infant mortality in Sweden: comparison with England and Wales. *BMJ* 1992; 305(19):687–91
30. Maxwell R. *International comparisons of health needs and services*. London: King's Fund Centre, 1980.

Quality in health care: getting to the heart of the matter

Fiona Moss
Editor, Quality in Health Care, *and Consultant Physician,*
Central Middlesex Hospital NHS Trust

'Assumptions are the things that you don't know you're making.'[1]

More people are harmed, and more unnecessary distress caused, by poor communication and uncoordinated, poorly organised health care than because a hospital lacks equipment. But while the headline 'No scanner at St Agnes – injured boy transferred' will inspire sponsored fun-runs to raise the necessary money, the headline 'No quality improvement programme at St Agnes – injured boy transferred' is unimaginable. Understanding the deficiencies of health care in terms of lack of technical and human resources is easy and it is possible, sometimes, to respond in kind. But the more potent causes of poor-quality care and harm are not so tangible and defy such clear-cut solutions. Quality improvement programmes are, of course, the solution that some would advocate. But they lack the cachet of new equipment and do not have obvious track records of success. So, what should we be doing about 'quality'.

What are the problems?

It is easy to find examples to illustrate deficiencies in the quality of health care. Most people have a tale to tell of difficulties experienced with the Health Service. Such experiences are not usually life-threatening but local and national newspapers keep us up to date with the more sensational mistakes and errors. Here I will describe briefly some examples that illustrate three broad areas of poor-quality care – problems with medico-technical aspects of care, problems with organisation and problems with communication.

From a medico-technical perspective there is plenty of published evidence – and certainly much more unpublished – to indicate on the one hand that some people do not receive treatments known to be effective, and on the other hand that some patients receive interventions inappropriately. Examples include the underuse of steroids in the treatment of acute severe asthma[2] and the underuse of ß blockers and aspirin following myocardial infarction – treatments associated with lower mortality and reduced morbidity; and the inappropriate use of coronary angiography and coronary artery surgery in the investigation and treatment of coronary artery disease.[3]

How a hospital or practice is organised and the people working in it are managed can affect the delivery of care. Poor organisation or inadequate supervision are direct causes of poor-quality health care. Most people either have themselves been challenged by or know someone who has experienced the long waits, the apparent disorganisation and administrative chaos that have come, sometimes unfairly, to characterise the NHS. *The Patient's Charter*[4] was an attempt to improve these problems. Mostly, disorganisation results in frustrating experiences for patients usually shouldered without complaint. But in some circumstances poor organisation and poor supervision are potentially dangerous and can cause harm – as, for example, described by the confidential enquiries into perioperative deaths (CEPOD) that revealed higher perioperative mortality when surgical procedures are done in inappropriate circumstances.[5]

Poor communication and lack of information engender anger and frustration – even when the technical aspects of care are good. And again are mostly not commented on by patients. But analysis of the problems that prompt people to seek redress for poor-quality care through litigation reveals that the majority of complaints about problems with clinical aspects of care include a complaint about communication.[6]

Improving most problems of health care will involve organisational change and new attitudes to patients and their needs. Small deficiencies in care may not seem to matter much, and may not be noticed in that singly they are unlikely to cause harm. But most serious errors are the consequence of a series of smaller minor faults in the system.

What is meant by good-quality care?

Good-quality health care is so much more than a measure of the technical aspects of clinical interventions. Much of health care is a series of compromises and trade-offs and choices made in the best circumstances by fully informed patients guided by knowledgeable health professionals in appropriate surroundings. Good-quality care also incorporates appropriate and competent technical care with opportunities for patients to make choices and to discuss concerns and anxieties, and it should result in an outcome appropriate to the problem. Even this long and cumbersome description excludes some of the important aspects of good-quality health care, such as fairness and access, and assumes much in the phrase 'competent technical care'.

One of Robert Maxwell's important contributions to the debate on the quality of health care, published in a paper that also emphasised the importance of the measurement and the use of reliable evidence for assessing quality, was to describe health care quality in terms of six dimensions (see Box 1).[7] Some of the original six have been renamed – perhaps the onomatopoeic mnemonic EEEAAR (see Box 2) could not be resisted – and in their various forms these dimensions have informed discussions about quality and, importantly, have influenced those who shape the delivery of health care. The six are not set in stone, and I would add three more – respect, choice and the provision of real information. These are to some extent subsumed in appropriateness[8] but in my view merit separate attention – particularly if some of the endemic problems associated with poor-quality care are to be resolved.

Box 1

- Access to health
- Relevance to need (for the whole community)
- Effectiveness (for individual patients)
- Equity (fairness)
- Social acceptability
- Efficiency and economy

By applying the six dimensions to each of the components of health care – structure, process and outcome – put forward by Donabedian as targets for quality assurance, Maxwell has demonstrated the construction of a matrix that can be used to ask a series of questions about the quality of care, for example in an intensive care unit (see Box 2 and Table 1).[9] From this matrix it is possible to get a view of many of the components of the quality of care. Change and improvement in some areas may require more resources. But others, such as compliance with protocols, record of explanations given to patients or looking for bias in admission policy, are aspects of care that could be improved through internal discussion and negotiation.

By using such a matrix it is possible more easily to understand and to encompass the relevance of health care quality beyond the care of the individual. In today's health care, professionals should not be blind to the needs of the population. The dimensions of quality help emphasise that quality is a function of care for the population as well as the individual.[9] For example, appropriate care has to be appropriate for an individual and take into account the population needs: a treatment for an individual that took up all resources and denied others treatment would be inappropriate.

Measurement and quality improvement

At the beginning of the paper in which he outlined the dimensions of quality Robert Maxwell makes a plea for methodical assessment in pursuit of better quality care. While remaining respectful of 'genuine, honest concern' about quality, he argued that – in 1984 – this was no longer enough.[7] An irony is that this plea has to be made to the medical profession – a profession that has for centuries based practice on measurement. In his play *The Herbal Bed* Peter Whelan gives John Hall, Shakespeare's son-in-law and herbalist, the line 'Exact quantity is the soul of practice'.

In contrast to measuring out milligrams, dispensing millilitres or counting pixels, measuring the quality of care is difficult. There simply is not an easy test for the quality of care. Without measurement not only is it difficult to appreciate problems with care and their causes

Table 1 Assessing quality in an intensive care unit

	Structure	Process	Outcome
Effectiveness	Staffing level and skills Equipment Access to theatres, etc.	Workload (volume of patients treated) Compliance with protocols, where relevant Data based peer review Infection and complications rates	Survival rates compared with similar units for matched cases
Acceptability	Is setting frightening or reassuring? What provision is there for relatives (privacy for counselling, overnight accommodation)?	Is explanation to relatives required and recorded in notes?	Is there follow up of patients and of relatives to obtain their opinions and suggestions for improvements?
Efficiency	Avoidance of extravagance in structure, equipment, and staffing	Throughput, staffing, etc. Admission and discharge arrangements	Costs for comparable cases
Access		How many patients suitable for admission have to be refused because the unit is full?	What actually happens to patients refused or delayed admission because the unit is full?
Equity		Is there any evidence of bias in who is admitted or how they are treated?	Is there any evidence of bias in outcomes?
Relevance	Bearing in mind other needs, is this service an appropriate use of resources at the current activity and expenditure level?		How much difference does the unit make to survival and health status, and for whom?

Source: Maxwell [9]

but also it is not possible easily to demonstrate good-quality care and its achievements. Institutional and professional failure to come to terms with the importance of measuring the quality of care in a systematic way should not be interpreted as being cavalier about the consequences of clinical interventions or uncaring attitudes. The apparent reluctance to grasp the necessity of methodical assessment of the quality of care may be because, 'genuine, honest concern' about and commitment to the care given to individual patients by clinical staff makes it difficult to conceive of systemic problems with the quality of care.

One of the effects of the medical and clinical audit programmes – about which more latter – was to encourage measurement of aspects of the quality of clinical care that have direct relevance to patient care. Encouraged by the audit directive, health care professionals began then systematically to assess care against standards. The frameworks provided by the Maxwell's dimensions of quality and Donabedian's description of the components of health care were important aids to those starting to measure the quality of care.

Measurement is central to quality improvement. But there are some caveats. Figures can be alluring. And attention naturally tends focus on those aspects of care that can be measured easily. This gives a distorted view of care, unless the measured part of care is considered alongside other aspects of the quality of care. An example is waiting-lists statistics. These are of course important and are one measure of access to care. But for some surgical interventions discussion about effectiveness and appropriateness is important too – and possibly relevant to the size of a waiting list; however, being more difficult to measure than numbers of people on waiting lists, they prompt less concern. 'Thousands of people on hospital waiting lists' is a much more compelling headline than 'There may be some people who don't need their operation'.

Second, measurement is not always needed to recognise problems – as any patient who has experienced poor quality will testify – just as in clinical practice there are some conditions that do not require investigations as the diagnosis and treatment are obvious without.

Chicken pox is diagnosed by observation of a rash not by electron microscopy of viral particles. In looking at problems of quality we need to develop that sort of diagnostic acumen. When the common and the obvious are spotted straightaway, they should be 'diagnosed' without resort to unnecessary measurement, and solutions found without fuss.

Third, the measurements should be simple and functional. Ideally, collection of data that will inform quality improvement should be part of routine practice and record-keeping. Finally, some aspects of quality are difficult to measure but may be very important. An example is equity. The Maxwell–Donabedian matrix enables these aspects of quality, even if not measured or formally assessed, at least to be acknowledged.

The essentials of quality improvement

Quality improvement is about change. After identification and measurement or assessment of a problem the steps that should lead to quality improvement are analysis of the cause and then implementation of change. But although these stages can be represented simply – as for example in the audit cycle – they encompass some very complex and difficult processes unfamiliar to many clinicians. Donald Berwick points out that the theoretical background of total quality management (TQM) comes from several disciplines, which include statistics, social psychology, industrial engineering and systems theory.[9] And of these only statistics has a high priority in medical school curricula.

Originating from the industrial and business world over 50 years ago, the principles of TQM have been written about extensively but have not been assimilated much into health care.[11] Briefly, these espouse a focus on customers; on measurement; on the working relationships within teams; on looking after – training and educating – staff; and on the principle that faults lie in the processes or systems of care and not in individual failure (see Box 3).[12] Donald Berwick has described TQM as a collection of approaches to efficiency, quality and leadership. He also outlines the 'new skills' that doctors and, by implication, other health care professionals need to acquire if

Box 3 Some characteristics of total quality management

- Defining quality in terms of customers' needs
- Making customers' needs a priority for everyone
- Recognising the existence of internal customers and suppliers
- Using sound measurement to understand how to improve quality
- Examining the process of care for explanation of poor quality
- Involving everyone on quality improvement
- Removing barriers between staff
- Promoting effective team working
- Promoting training for everyone
- Understanding that quality improvement is a continuous process

Source: Moss & Garside [12]

Box 4 'New clinical skills' of quality management

- Ability to perceive and work effectively in interdependencies
- Ability to work in teams
- Ability to understand work as a process
- Skills in collection, aggregation and analysis of outcome data
- Skills in 'designing' health care practices
- Skills in collection, aggregation and analysis of data on processes of work
- Skills in collaborative exchange with patients
- Skills in collaborative exchange with lay managers

Source: Berwick et al. [13]

quality improvement is to become integrated into health care (see Box 4).[10,13] The implications of this list and the label 'new' skills challenge some of the assumptions about how health care is, in reality, often practised. Many will assume that they work well in teams and do have 'collaborative exchange' with patients. But anyone who wants an honest perspective on how well their teams work should ask their customers.

Understanding work as a process is crucial for effective quality improvement. The process of a single episode of care for any patient within the hospital system will depend on the co-operation and interdependencies of many people from several groups. For example,

le will be involved either directly or indirectly in the
atient in a district hospital undergoing outpatient
.... and assessment of operability for a probable lung
cancer. The list includes receptionists and secretaries and pathology
technicians as well as consultants and nurse practitioners. Each person
has an important role in enabling the patient to receive appropriate,
skilful and co-ordinated care. The processes of care extend even
further if the primary care team and the tertiary care team, and the
patient's family, are included. But from the patient's perspective
care does not separate neatly into the separate groups that provide
each part. Getting co-ordination right and making sure that everyone
understands enough about the other parts of the process so each can
provide useful accurate information is obviously important.
Any attempt to improve the quality of care even for those aspects of
care that are primarily clinical requires co-operation between many
people.

Looked at from without the context of routine clinical practice the
essentials of quality improvement seem to make good organisational
sense. Take for example the principle of promoting effective team
working. The opposite of this would be care by individuals not working
together as a team and would result in poor communication and
other characteristics of dysfunctional teams. Similarly, the converse
of putting the needs of customers (patients) as a priority for everyone
is clearly absurd. But the point is that at least at times and in some
circumstances that is how the health service is seen to operate. If a
way could be found formally to incorporate the principles of quality
improvement, this could make a difference to the delivery of health
care possibly far beyond the impact of a new scanner.

The process of implementing change, even on a small scale, is far from
straightforward, as illustrated by the experiences of those who have
attempted to introduce guidelines. Many ways to influence change
in clinical practice have been proposed – educational; behavioural;
organisational; social interaction; coercive; epidemiological; and
marketing. Each has its own underlying theory and particular group
of proponents.[14,15] There is much yet to be determined about changing
clinical practice and clearly no approach is the only or the best way.

The essential skills of quality improvement provide a context that may make change easier. But the enormity of any change needed for those skills to be acquired should not be underestimated.

Moving towards quality improvement in the NHS

There is a huge gap between the rhetoric of quality improvement and the reality of how we practise health care – despite the common sense of the principles of quality improvement. But within the NHS there have undoubtedly been some changes and a growing awareness of the many components of good-quality care.

In the UK quality improvement has taken shape largely through audit. Medical audit was included in the 1990 NHS reforms as one of seven key changes and supported with about £50 million each year of ring-fenced moneys. At first inclusive only of doctors, audit was subsequently extended via the clinical audit programme to include other health care professionals. Many have doubted the efficacy of the audit programme and have suggested that the £250 million invested in audit programmes was not a good use of public money.

The extraordinary features of the NHS audit programme were that it involved the near-mandatory introduction of a programme designed to improve the quality of care and a process that involved internal reflection rather than a system of external inspection and that it was supported financially. This was an unprecedented set of conditions. And although no system was set up prospectively to assess its impact on the delivery of care, there have been some important changes attributable to the audit programme.

The audit programme certainly introduced clinicians to the task of measuring the quality of care. Measurement is a crucial first step, although alone is unlikely to improve the quality of care. Many hospitals now measure, for example, the time taken for patients with acute myocardial infarction to receive thrombolytic therapy;[16] know the number of patients who, following a myocardial infarction and suitable for treatment with ß blockers and aspirin, actually get these drugs; and know the number of patients admitted with acute severe asthma treated with oral steroids.[17] This information is mostly collected not for the purpose of publishing papers but for local use as part of the audit process and can be found in the 'grey literature' of trust annual audit reports and in the (old) Regional Audit reports. Collection of this sort of information was not a regular feature of clinical practice before the introduction of audit. This has been a quiet but significant revolution.

Getting 'stuck' at the stage of measurement ended many audits without producing change[18] and probably contributed to loss of enthusiasm with audit. But in retrospect, this was perhaps not unexpected, as the documents and papers published at the start of the audit programmes contained relatively little advice or information about either how to look at the processes of care to determine the cause of problems identified through measurement or about the complex process of change.

The ultimate aim of any quality improvement programme in health care must be to improve the care given to patients. And despite the constrains on the way audit was set up and introduced, we can be confident that patients have benefited. The overall contribution of audit to patient care cannot be quantified, but at the very least, many small improvements in patient care have been identified in many hospitals and practices. In places where there has been some progress from audit towards a more organisationally based approach to quality improvement there may have been more lasting change. For example, at Central Middlesex Hospital, London, the use of ß blockers and aspirin following myocardial infarction increased from 78 to 96 per cent of all eligible patients by changing from separate medical and nursing records to a single patient record. The new record, used by the whole team, incorporates an agreed protocol for care of patients with myocardial infarction that includes essential steps in management. This protocol is always available at the bedside to all those concerned with the patient's care. Before discharge the patient's nurse checks to establish whether ß blockers and aspirin have been prescribed.[19] This sort of change requires time and much collaboration between medical and nursing staff and effective teamworking.

The achievements of audit can also be assessed in the context of the complex and difficult processes that are needed for an approach to quality improvement that really puts customers first, develops all staff and encourages good teamwork. Audit may have been a useful a preliminary step in the development of those organisational changes. The move from medical to clinical audit was itself a step that should not be underestimated.

An evaluation of the audit programme in 29 provider units identified the organisational characteristics associated with effective audit programmes. These included the audit staff themselves, the leadership and direction, and the level of strategic planning for audit. It was also noted that the more effective audit programmes were in those places where audit resources had been invested mostly in staff and the demands for heavy investment in information technology had been resisted.[20] It seems possible that those organisations where audit was most effective were those most developed in the direction of quality improvement.

Re-reading some of the papers and documents written about audit seven years ago , I am aware now of a change in attitudes to audit and to quality and also the development of a greater ease of use of the language and understanding of the principles of quality improvement. For example, both the anxiety expressed by many doctors at the start of the medical audit programme about discussing poor quality of care discovered through audit outside 'doctor only' groups, and concern about the confidentiality of audit data now seem dated.

It is not clear what was expected of the medical and clinical audit programmes. Their introduction was not based on the sort of evidence that clinical professionals are used to – a randomised trial or pilot evaluation. And the introduction of NHS-wide quality improvement initiatives could be considered an 'act of faith'. Some have argued that clinical audit should have been considered an 'emergent technology' and appropriately assessed before introduction.[21] Despite the lack of pre-testing or robust prospective evaluation, the audit programme with its limitations may have helped shape an environment in which at least some health care professionals in some places are eager to acquire the 'new' skills essential for quality improvement. Audit may yet prove to have been a sound long-term investment.

Quality improvement: the next steps

Papers on the quality of care almost invariably only discuss poor-quality care and how to do things better. So, before finishing I want to acknowledge that much care with in the NHS is good and that some people do get a very good deal. But there are endemic problems that reduce efficiency and limit effectiveness, that cannot be blamed on lack of resources. Poorly communicated, poorly organised, uncoordinated care are rather a reflection of how health care professionals work together.

In addition to setting out the 'new' essential skills for quality improvement, Donald Berwick set out four barriers to the acquisition of these skills (see Box 5).[13] There is an uncomfortable familiarity about this list that points to some of the unattractive characteristics of professionalism. We assume that we work well in teams; that we are unaffected by disputes over professional territory; that we trust colleagues from other professions; and that we hold onto only the positive aspects of tradition. The philosophy of continuous quality improvement runs counter to the tribalism of health care; its messages are awkward and do not fit neatly into the traditional professional model. In a recent editorial Robert Maxwell with others challenges the medical and other health care professions to review aspects of their professional bargain with society. One of these is '[to become] more willing to develop partnerships with other caring professions and to allow greater flexibility in working practice to improve patient care'.[22]

There is a choice. We can recognise that new, flexible patterns of working with a greater emphasis on communication and provision of information are crucial if care is to become genuinely more responsive to patients and free from unnecessary and ultimately costly deficiencies. Or, we can maintain the professional *status quo*

Box 5 Barriers to participation in managing quality

- Time
- Territory
- Tradition
- Trust

Source: Berwick et al.[13]

and become increasingly out of touch with patients. The problems in health care are not new but recent changes in the patterns of care – an increase in primary care, short stay and ambulatory care – and increased public expectations are further reasons for looking critically at how we work. Quality improvement is largely a matter of organisational change and understanding. Even those areas of quality improvement that seem to relate primarily to clinical matters are likely to require an organisational or managerial imperative for real changes to happen. And any change is likely to need the co-operation of more than one group or tribe. In short, good quality health care assumes a high degree of interdependency and teamworking. If quality improvement is to be at the heart of health care, then we need a 'new professionalism'. That is, a professionalism that ignores the old tribal boundaries and that encompasses the 'new skills'. The health care professions have different and distinct functions. These are crucial. But all health professions need to examine working practices and traditions and find ways of working flexibly and in genuine teams. This will be a sure way of improving patient care. Our patients should demand nothing less of us.

References
1. Adams D, Carwardine M. *Last chance to see ...* Oxford: Heinemann, 1990.
2. Bucknall CE, Robertson C, Moran F, Stephenson RD. Differences in hospital asthma management. *Lancet* 1988; i:748–50.
3. Gray D, Hampton J, Bernstein S, Kosekoff J, Brooks R. Audit of coronary angiography and bypass surgery. *Lancet* 1990; 335:1317–20.
4. Department of Health. *The patient's charter*. London: HMSO, 1991.

5. Buck N, Devlin H, Lunn J. *The report of a confidential enquiry into perioperative deaths*. London: Nuffield Provincial Hospital Trust, 1988.
6. Bark P, Vincent C, Jones A, Savory J. Clinical complaints: a means of improving the quality of care. *Quality in Health Care* 1994; 3:123–32.
7. Maxwell R. Quality assessment in health. *BMJ* 1984; 288:1470–2.
8. Hopkins A. What do we mean by appropriate health care? Report of a working group unprepared for the Director of Research and Development of the NHS management executive. *Quality in Health Care* 1993; 2:117–23.
9. Maxwell R. Dimensions of quality revisited: from thought to action. *Quality in Health Care* 1992; 1:171–7.
10. Berwick D, Enthoven A, Bunker JP. Quality management in the NHS: the doctor's role – 1. *BMJ* 1992; 304:235–9.
11. Pollitt C. Business approaches to quality improvement: why are they hard for the NHS to swallow? *Quality in Health Care* 1996; 5:104–10.
12. Moss F, Garside P. The importance of quality. In: Simpson J, Smith R (eds). *Management for doctors*. London: BMJ Publishing, 1995.
13. Berwick D, Enthoven A, Bunker JP. Quality management in the NHS: the doctor's role. *BMJ* 1992; 304:304–8.
14. Grol R. Beliefs and evidence in changing clinical practice. *BMJ* 1997; 315:418–21.
15. Robertson N, Baker R, Hearnshaw H. Changing the clinical behaviour of doctors: a psychological framework. *Quality in Health Care* 1996; 5:51–4.
16. Nee PA, Gray AJ, Martin MA. Audit of thrombolysis initiated in an accident and emergency department. *Quality in Health Care* 1994; 3:29–33.
17. Pearson MG, Ryland I, Harrison BD. National audit of acute severe asthma in adults admitted to hospital. *Quality in Health Care* 1995; 4:24–30.
18. Crombie IK, Davies HTO. Missing link in the audit cycle. *Quality in Health Care* 1993; 2:47–8.
19. Layton A, Alimo A, Riordan J. Personal communication
20. Buttery Y, Walshe K, Rumney M, Amess M, Bennett J, Coles J. *Evaluating audit. Provider audit in England. A review of 29 programmes*. London: CASPE Research, 1995.
21. Buxton M. Achievements of audit in the NHS. *Quality in Health Care* 1994; 3:s31–4.
22. Abelson J, Maxwell PH, Maxwell RJ. Do the professions have a future? Perhaps, if they are not defensive or complacent. *BMJ* 1997; 315:382.

Keeping pace with advanced research

First years of the Nuffield Council on Bioethics

The Rt Hon Sir Patrick Nairne GCB MC
Former Chairman, Nuffield Council on Bioethics

A conference of the great and the good was held at Cumberland Lodge on the weekend of 20–22 April 1990. The Nuffield Foundation was the host; its Chairman, Lord Flowers, presided. The main theme of the conference was formidable. What, if anything, should be done in response to the ethical problems clearly, even alarmingly, posed by the rapid developments in medical and biological research? Was the human race being left behind by advances in research?

Establishing the Nuffield Council on Bioethics

Robert Maxwell attended; the occasion would have been incomplete without him. I do not recall what he had to say. He may perhaps have been sceptical, as some were at the outset, about the value of what was proposed: the establishment of a body of professional and academic standing with the role of producing reports – of which the Government might take little or no notice – on what could prove complex and controversial issues. Be that as it may, the conference concluded that a national body of the kind envisaged should be set up. Eight months later, after extensive consultation, the Trustees of the Nuffield Foundation established the Nuffield Council on Bioethics with the following terms of reference:

1. To identify and define ethical questions raised by recent advances in biological and medical research in order to respond to, and to anticipate, public concern.
2. To make arrangements for examining and reporting on such questions with a view to promoting public understanding and discussion; this may lead, where needed, to the formulation of new guidelines by the appropriate regulatory or other body.
3. In the light of the outcome of its work, to publish reports; and to make representations, as the Council may judge appropriate.

The creation of the new Council was not as easy as that suggests. Pressure had been growing from those engaged in advanced medical research for some action to be taken. That may have been partly fall-out from the Warnock Report, leading to greater awareness of ethical factors in research. More specifically, there was the influential voice of Professor Sir David Weatherall, then Nuffield Professor of Clinical Medicine at Oxford, expressing serious concern that advances in biomedical research were running dangerously ahead of our understanding of their implications for our lives. What, it could be asked, did geneticists know about how individuals would react to being told that they had a genetic predisposition for developing cancer or heart disease in 20 years' time? Xenografts were the subject of research, but was any thought being given to the ethical aspects of research relating to animal-to-human transplants?

Hence the conference case for a national body. *But what kind of body, and who should set it up?* The possibility had been explored of persuading the Government to establish a standing body, analogous perhaps to the Royal Commission on Environmental Pollution. But Whitehall was unwilling to respond. Lord Flowers had had to recognise that, if there was to be a national body, the Nuffield Foundation itself would have to create it.

The Trustees encountered reservations from the Medical Research Council, which argued that *ad hoc* bodies had proved effective in the past and would be preferable to a standing body. But the general response to a consultation memorandum, sent to some 175 organisations and about 60 individuals, had been generally encouraging; and the determination of Lord Flowers and the support, in particular, of Sir David Weatherall and Dame Margaret Turner-Warwick, President of the Royal College of Physicians, carried the day. The Nuffield Council on Bioethics was established – warmly welcomed by the Prime Minister when it was reported to him – and on 26 July 1991 it held its first meeting at the Nuffield Foundation. It was composed of 15 members (see Figure 1), the majority unconnected with biomedical research, and included Sir David and Dame Margaret. At the insistence of Lord Flowers, I agreed to chair the Council.

The ethics of genetic screening

Where should the Council start?

The range of ethical issues, arising from *advances* in biomedical and biological science, had increased in scale and complexity: the choice was wide. But, after surveying the field, the Council quickly agreed that advances in genetic research and, in particular, genetic screening should be its first priority.

Rt Hon Sir Patrick Nairne – Chairman
Mrs Beverly Anderson
Miss Margaret Auld
Professor Canon Gordon Dunstan
Professor John Gurdon
Professor Eve Johnstone
Professor Ian Kennedy
Dr Anne McLaren
Mrs Caroline Miles
Dr Brian Newbould
Dr Onora O'Neill
Miss Jane Reed
Professor Dame Margaret Turner-Warwick
Professor Sir David Weatherall
Professor Sir David Williams

Figure 1 Nuffield Council on Bioethics – as established in June 1991

How should it do its work?

The Council decided to appoint for its genetic screening inquiry – as it was to do for subsequent inquiries – a working party under an external chairman, Professor Dame June (now Baroness) Lloyd, with a membership of relevant expertise and experience, including two members of the Council. The working party would carry out its exacting task within a framework agreed by the Council, but would be free to consult as widely as it wished. As became established Council practice, the working party chairman would join in discussions with the Council at the delicate stage of submitting the draft report, and would then partner the Council chairman in presenting the report to the media. Members of both the working party and the Council would be able, in different ways, to play a part in conveying the message of the report to government and professional authorities, and to the general public. As a procedure this worked well.

Genetic screening was not a completely new field; it had long been practised in applying phenylketonuria (PKU) tests to newborn babies, and pilot studies had been started for cystic fibrosis. But recent developments in genetic research had now caught the attention of the media and the public. Typical headlines had ranged from

'Women face agonising choice over genetic breast test' to 'Genetic tests threaten to create underclass'. Thus serious fears could be aroused and formidable dilemmas posed: 'Do I want a test to tell me that I have inherited the gene for a serious disease for which there is no known cure or adequate therapy?' And yet it is the genetic field which is likely to offer the most effective route to the causes and mechanisms of many serious diseases; and progress in research depends on people voluntarily participating in screening programmes. Wider public understanding and practical guidelines for genetic screening were, therefore, recognised by the Council as urgent ethical requirements.

Report on genetic screening

The Council endorsed the working party report and published it in December 1993. The report made clear the hopes, fears and potential benefits attached to genetic screening; it explained the importance of pilot screening studies for monogenic diseases, and of the international human genome project, which could lead in due course to widespread genetic screening, including the even more difficult field of polygenic diseases. Against this background the report concluded that:

- there is an urgent need for effective and acceptable ethical safeguards, standards and procedures relating to informed consent, counselling, confidentiality and the prevention of unjustifiable discrimination in employment and insurance;
- there is a parallel need to stimulate wide public discussion about the social and ethical implications of genetic screening;
- in particular, adequately informed consent and counselling should be a prior requirement for all participants in genetic screening programmes; confidential account should be taken of the wider *family implications* of individual screening results; confidentiality should be effectively preserved, especially in using genetic registers; and *a central co-ordinating body* should be set up to review genetic screening programmes and to monitor their operation and results, drawing upon the stringent criteria set out in the report.

The Government was also recommended to keep under review the potential use of genetic screening by employers, for which legislation might eventually be needed. More urgent action, however, was recommended to deal with the special problems relating to insurance. Although the potential importance of genetic test data to insurers was fully recognised, the insurance companies were urged not to change their current test policies, and to accept a temporary moratorium on requiring the disclosure of genetic data pending the outcome of discussions between the Government and the insurance industry. This recommendation was directly discussed with both the Department of Health and the Association of British Insurers, emphasising its importance to all those linking personal insurance to a house mortgage.

The report received a good press. The important implications, for individuals and for society, of success in genetic research, the measures required on ethical grounds and the particular problem of insurance were given wide publicity. The report was also discussed with some professional authorities, and informal contacts were made with some Members of Parliament. But Government action was slow to come. It was, therefore, a welcome step when, in November 1994, the Science and Technology Committee of the House of Commons announced that it was initiating an inquiry into 'Human genetics: the science and its consequences'.

Inquiry by the Science and Technology Committee

The Committee summoned many witnesses, including the Nuffield Council, relevant interest groups and individual experts; it also visited key institutes, centres and authorities in the USA and the European Union as well as in the UK. It published its report in July 1995 with an impressive range of recommendations. The most important recommendation related to the establishment of a Human Genetics Commission, with a role which included monitoring developments in genetics and advising the Government; approving screening programmes; overseeing the effect of genetic medicine on the insurance market and on employment; keeping under review the law and practice of patenting; recommending research programmes; and encouraging public education and debate. In short, Parliament had published an admirable report which the Government could not ignore.

In slow time a White Paper emerged, followed by the announcement in January 1996 of an Advisory Committee on Genetic Testing, complementing an earlier committee, the Advisory Committee on Gene Therapy set up in 1993. The Committee of Science and Technology sought oral evidence from Stephen Dorrell, then Secretary of State for Health. That led to further Government action. In December 1996 – exactly three years after publication of the Nuffield Council report – the establishment of the Human Genetics Advisory Commission was announced. Chaired by Sir Colin Campbell, Vice-Chancellor of Nottingham University, it includes among its members Dr Onora O'Neill, now Chairman of the Nuffield Council. Its tasks are to consider 'the broad social, ethical, and/or economic consequences of developments in human genetics, for example, in relation to public health, insurance, patents and employment' and to 'advise on ways to build public confidence in the new science'. The topical issue of cloning has been included in the Commission's agenda, on which the insurance implications of the new genetics have a priority place.

Where are we now?

Public policy has been developing slowly, while genetic research races on. How far have screening programmes been developed? Have the recommended ethical safeguards and procedures been adopted? Will concerns about insurance be adequately met? Is the general public better informed? Impossible to know; perhaps still premature to ask. But essential first steps have been taken and monitoring and advisory arrangements are in place. The Nuffield Council, for its part, is again at work in the genetic field. A working party, chaired by Dame Fiona Caldicott, former President of the Royal College of Psychiatrists, is now inquiring into the ethical issues relating to the genetics of mental disorders.

Human tissue – ethical and legal issues

The second report of the Nuffield Council, published in April 1995, was entitled: *Human tissue – ethical and legal issues*. The subject had been proposed at the very first meeting of the Council – when the question had been asked: 'But does it raise any *new* ethical questions? Is it not mainly questions of law?'. The fact is that it involves both types of question. Their background was summarised in the opening paragraph of the Council's report of April 1995 – produced by a working party chaired by Professor Dame Rosalind Hurley:

> One aspect of the recent and rapid advances in biological and medical research is that human tissue is being used in an increasing variety of new ways. Many of these developments ... have unquestionable benefits; but using human tissue in different ways also raises questions of law and presents new ethical dilemmas.

That last sentence was strikingly illustrated in the case of *Moore* v *Regents of the University of California*. It is a story worth telling.

Case of Mr John Moore

In Autumn 1976 a Mr John Moore was told at the UCLA Medical Center that he had a rare form of leukaemia. The diagnosis was confirmed by removing blood, bone marrow aspirate, and other bodily substances, which the doctors recognised at that time would provide (to quote the judgment of the Supreme Court of California) 'competitive, commercial, and scientific advantages'. Moore signed a written consent form for the removal of his spleen, portions of which were then sent to a research unit *without* his being either told or asked to consent. On medical advice, he returned to the UCLA Medical Center several times between November 1976 and September 1983; on each occasion samples of tissue were removed and used for research, to the prospective financial benefit of Moore's doctors. In due course this research enabled a cell line to be established, a patent to be issued, and agreements negotiated for its commercial development – with the prospect of substantial benefit for both the doctors and the University. Eventually all this became known to Moore. He took legal action in 1984, claiming wrongful interference

194

with another's property and lack of informed consent. His case ended up in the Supreme Court of California, which reached an important majority decision: Moore had *no* property rights in cells taken from his body. The issue of whether the doctors had been in breach of their duty towards Moore, in particular the failure to obtain his consent, was remitted for trial, but was settled out of court.

The Moore case was exceptional, but within it can be found – as briefly explained below – *all* the principal ethical issues which can arise from the uses of human tissue.

It is rare for human tissue removed for medical treatment to be of any research interest; but certain forms of tissue *can* sometimes offer valuable research potential, as shown by the samples from Moore. Is it now accepted that a patient has no claim on any subsequent financial benefit? Moore's medical treatment was not prejudiced, and for that the ethical requirement of consent was met. But should that consent now be taken to cover the subsequent use of a patient's tissue? It is an ethical requirement that no commercial considerations should affect either the acquisition or the donation of tissue, since they could damage the relationship of trust between doctor and patient – as they did with Moore. On the other hand, the commercial development of patient tissue may be for the benefit of medicine generally, and financial transactions may be unavoidable. Is it enough to rely on altruistic donation if tissue that can save lives is in short supply? A cell line derived from Moore was patented, since presumably the criteria for patentability had been met; but ethical factors must also be recognised in patenting inventions derived from human tissue.

The removal of tissue

Thus the ethical factors are complex. Why was it judged that John Moore had no property rights over his own tissue when, exceptionally, it proved to be commercially valuable? The Nuffield Council report explained the present position:

English law is silent on the issue of whether a person can claim a property right in tissue which has been removed. The traditional view has been that a body is not property ... The question remains open ... whether in certain circumstances the English courts would uphold the claim of someone from whom tissue had been removed ... The likely approach would be that, where tissue is removed in the course of treatment, consent to the treatment will entail the abandonment of any claim to the tissue.

The report added:

At common law, the issue has not been tested in English law. It is instructive to enquire why the question of a claim over tissue once removed has not received legal attention. The answer seems simple. In the general run of things a person from whom tissue is removed has not the slightest interest in making any claim to it once it is removed.

The issues of consent and claims may continue to be controversial as productive research and the development of tissue banks grow in scope and scale; but what the Nuffield Council recommended appears to be accepted without challenge – if only because of the difficult problems which any rights of patients to make claims in property would be likely to create:

We recommend that the law should proceed on any claim over removed tissue by examining the basis of the consent given to the procedure that resulted in the removal of tissue. In particular, it should be regarded as entailed in consent to medical treatment that tissue removed ... will be regarded as having been abandoned by the person from whom it was removed.

The report consequently recommended that consent procedures and the text of forms should be carefully reviewed.

Commercial considerations

But that recommendation – which does not mention the possibility of any claim if patient tissue should prove valuable – was complemented by a further recommendation. Tissue removed in the course of treatment should be specifically regarded as *abandoned*, thus reflecting the implication of the Acts relating to human tissue, anatomy and human organs, of 1961, 1984 and 1989 respectively, that tissue removed is given as an unconditional gift. Underlying that recommendation is the ethical principle of altruism, which was strongly upheld by the Nuffield Council, together with the view that, notwithstanding the increased importance of commercial factors in the NHS, there should be no *direct* commercial dealings in human tissue. It was recommended that hospitals and doctors should act only as intermediaries when commercial organisations are necessarily involved – for example, in manufacturing and distributing blood products.

In the Nuffield Council's view, a market for procuring human tissue might obstruct, rather than facilitate, informed consent when tissue removed in medical treatment is abandoned or in the special circumstances of tissue donation. The altruistic desire *to give,* in order to save the lives of others, should not be put at risk by any incentive payments. A market system might also lead to morally unacceptable or even criminal methods of procuring human tissue.

Commercial considerations are necessarily involved in patenting inventions derived from human tissue; and the granting of patents can be a significant factor in fostering investment in biotechnology. But there must be ethical limits to what is accepted as patentable; the acceptability, for example, of patenting human genes or transgenic animals, such as oncomouse, has been widely questioned. The Nuffield Council recommended that the Government should join its European partners in seeking a protocol to the European Patent Convention which would define ethical criteria for excluding from patentability unacceptable proposals relating to human and animal tissue. Further progress appears now to depend on the European Commission and European Parliament.

More could be written about the ethical and legal aspects of the uses of human tissue, and also about the difficulty of promoting public understanding of the key issues discussed above. While those issues affect us all, the report's recommendations are primarily for the

Government, NHS authorities and those working in health care. For them the widely circulated report offers an important basis for action and timely guidance of continuing value.

Animal-to-human transplants: the ethics of xenotransplantation

Xenotransplantation, to which the Council turned in 1995, presented issues of an entirely different kind. The Council's report in the following year put the case for an inquiry in its opening words:

> Rare attempts have made to transplant animal organs or tissue into human beings since the early years of this century. Interest in this procedure, known as xenotransplantation, has increased in the last few years because it is seen as one way of reducing the shortage of human organs for transplantation. Currently, this shortage severely limits the potential of transplantation for treating human disease. The prospect of using animal organs and tissue for xenotransplantation raises important issues, both practical and ethical, which must be debated ...

The Council was aware that, in 1994, the King's Fund Institute had published a report, *A question of give and take*, on 'improving the supply of donor organs for transplantation.' This had referred, though cautiously, to the option of xenotransplantation, foreshadowing the Nuffield Council study with references to the genetically engineered pig and associated ethical issues.

Problems posed by xenotransplantation

The Nuffield Council established a working party under the chairmanship of Professor Albert Weale of the University of Essex. It conducted a thorough study, recognising that the issues – both practical and ethical – had recently become more serious and urgent in the light of the increasing shortfall in human organ donation, the potential risk that xenografts might transmit new diseases, and public concern about the welfare of genetically modified animals. These concerns were given greater force by another factor. In September 1995 the UK company Imutran Ltd announced that, as a result of its research with pigs and monkeys, the first xenotransplantation of transgenic pig hearts into human patients might take place as early as 1996.

The working party's report, endorsed by the Council, began by highlighting the reason for an inquiry into xenotransplantation: a waiting list of 5000 or more for kidney transplants and approaching 400 for heart transplants. After summarising the ethical concerns which xenotransplantation aroused, the report reviewed the alternative options, notably artificial and bioengineered organs. It carefully considered the practical questions, showing them to be as crucial as the ethical ones. Could the problem of organ rejection be resolved? If ethical objections were considered to rule out the use of chimpanzees or baboons, could genetic modification ensure that rejection would be prevented if pigs were used? If there is inescapable uncertainty about the possible transmission of infectious diseases, must that uncertainty be assessed as a serious risk?

The report discussed the ethical problems at length. It engaged in public and professional consultation and was in contact with about 100 individuals and organisations. It drew on the substantial report of 1991 by the Institute of Medical Ethics, *Lives in the balance: the ethics of using animals in biomedical research*. It considered, as fully as possible, the ethical and more personal implications for patients, and for action in the NHS.

Report on xenotransplantation

The working party concluded that, since xenotransplantation offered the prospect of saving human lives and improving their quality, xenograft development should proceed – though cautiously. In view particularly of the potential benefit to patients, whose lives would otherwise remain at serious risk, the breeding of pigs to supply organs for xenotransplantation would be ethically justified. But there was another, and much more difficult, factor – the serious public health risk which could be posed by infectious organisms of animals. The working party recommended that an Advisory Committee on Xenotransplantation should be immediately established in order to assess that risk and to lay down the essential precautionary measures before any clinical human trials could be held. All the necessary safeguards had to be in place before xenotransplantation was offered to patients – and then only on the basis of strict ethical procedures relating to consent, and with research commissioned to study the impact on patients.

The Council report was generally well received. The case for developing safe and effective xenotransplantation was fully acknowledged. The ethical conclusions – assisted perhaps by the initial public consultation – were accepted without serious challenge. The potential risk of transmitted infection emerged as the immediate problem of greatest importance. It may have been that risk, reinforced by rising political concern and the pace at which Imutran was apparently proceeding, that led the Government – taking the Nuffield Council by surprise – to set up another inquiry of its own.

This further inquiry was conducted by the Advisory Group on the Ethics of Xenotransplantation, of which Professor Ian Kennedy, a member of the Nuffield Council, was appointed Chairman. The conclusions of his report of January 1997, *Animal tissue into humans*, were broadly in step with those of the Nuffield Council, though even more cautious in tone, and included complementary recommendations on the effective control of xenotransplantation. Armed with that report, the Government announced in March 1997 the establishment of the UK Xenotransplantation Interim Regulatory Authority under the chairmanship of Lord Habgood.

The role of the Authority is to advise on the action required for regulating xenotransplantation, covering safety, efficacy, research and the acceptability of specific applications. The Authority will be made statutory as soon as time can be found for legislation. Meanwhile, xenotransplantation remains a topic of continuing public interest and concern; and international efforts are being devoted to the introduction of common standards, particularly related to the risk of new infections. Imutran has not, at least for the time being, proceeded to clinical trials.

Questions in conclusion

This has been a summary account of the Nuffield Council's first five years. Has the Council effectively met the needs identified by the Cumberland Lodge conference? As defined in the consultation memorandum of 1990, those needs provide a checklist for the Council's performance:

- *'The need ... for a body that could survey the whole field of bioethics.'* The Council has regularly surveyed the field when considering its future agenda. Its reports reflect a wide range of issues.
- *'The need ideally to anticipate, or at least to respond with speed to, new bioethical problems'.* The report on xenotransplantation offers the best example of meeting that need.
- *'The need for a national UK voice... in European bioethics discussions.'* The Executive Secretary, David Shapiro, together with Council members, has played a valuable part.
- *'A national body ... to stimulate greater co-ordination in matters of bioethics both within Government and between the non-governmental bodies concerned.'* The Council's reports have necessarily led to some co-ordination between Whitehall Departments.
- *'A national body would also place bioethical issues higher on the public agenda.'* Quite apart from the media attention which each report has received, the Government's establishment of advisory bodies in the genetics field, and both a committee and an authority on xenotransplantation, show that bioethical issues are firmly on 'the public agenda'.

Thus the Council's terms of reference are being effectively fulfilled, though with one qualification. The promotion of 'public understanding and discussion' was an important element of the Council's remit; and that meant more than securing maximum media cover when its reports were published. As it has turned out, however, the Council itself, with its small secretariat, has never had the time or resources to stimulate wide public debate – though it has recently been able to do more with young people through discussions of xenotransplantation.

Achievements of the Nuffield Council

But what has the Nuffield Council actually achieved? It cannot be enough to point to three substantial reports. There is no easy or precise answer; but three claims could be made:

First, *questions of bioethics* have now secured a more prominent place in government policies and Parliamentary discussions; and the public is now alive to ethical issues which may affect us all. This has been largely due to the Council reports and subsequent action by Parliament and the Government.

Second, the Nuffield Council can claim at least a share of the credit for *stimulating Government action* on genetic screening and xenotransplantation. The Government had given a lead in establishing, in November 1989, the Clothier Committee on the Ethics of Gene Therapy; but a convincing need emerged for the wider terms of reference given to the Nuffield Council. The Council report and its oral evidence on genetic screening made a significant contribution to the inquiry into 'Human Genetics: the Science and its consequences' by the Parliamentary Science and Technology Committee. The Government's eventual action in establishing the two new advisory bodies – on genetic screening and, more widely, on developments in human genetics – clearly resulted from the valuable work of the Parliamentary Committee. The establishment of the Kennedy Committee was the Government's reaction to Imutran's announcement of progress in research, but that Committee's report drew on the Council's work, and it led to the Habgood Interim Authority – a broadly similar body to the committee which the Council had recommended almost a year earlier.

Third, there are *the reports* themselves. Some reports require instant action and, when that has been taken, their shelf life may be limited. If the Habgood Interim Authority receives statutory powers and implements gradually the measures recommended by the two reports on *xenotransplantation*, the Council's report may be filed as historical background to an established policy. That could eventually be true for the Council's report on *genetic screening*, but certainly not yet.

The *special importance* of the report, and of the Advisory Committee on Genetic Testing, lies in the special importance of screening programmes to the progress of genetic research . The recommended procedures for counselling, consent, and confidentiality need to be implemented, and the insurance issues resolved, before participants in screening programmes can be adequately safeguarded. The report on *human tissue*, however, is somewhat different. Its ethical and legal guidance may establish it as a standard work for the foreseeable future, while the uses of tissue continue to increase, tissue banks are being established, and the authorities need guidance on the relevant principles and practices.

A final question

There is a final question. *Would it have been better if the Council had been established by the Government?* In those countries where they exist, bodies analogous to the Nuffield Council have normally been established by governments.

The practical process of setting up a council on bioethics, with members of high calibre, and of appointing working parties, undertaking inquiries and publishing reports would be little different; and such a council would be free to formulate its own conclusions and recommendations. If the Government had established, and was funding, it (and was exposed to Parliamentary and media questions about it), ministers would be likely to respond more quickly to its recommendations, as the previous Government did after the Kennedy report on xenotransplantation. A Government council would also be a more appropriate focus of contact on bioethical issues with other Governments than an independent body like the Nuffield Council – which other countries have occasionally assumed to be a British Government body.

In short, a council appointed by the Government might enjoy some practical advantages. It would be different from the Nuffield Council only because of its position within the framework of government. That could, however, be a significant factor. At least in theory, a council appointed by the Government would be exposed to such *possibilities* as a ministerial decision not to publish a report, tight departmental control over the public presentation of reports, and even a government decision to abolish the council against its chairman's advice.

But those possibilities, and there could be others, are less important than another factor – a factor which demonstrates the importance of independent initiatives in the voluntary sector. The Nuffield Council was set up when – and because – it became clear that the Government had no intention of establishing a body with a wide role of inquiry in the field of bioethics. The Nuffield Foundation stepped in, consulted widely, and then proceeded to meet what had emerged as a national need. And the Council, working outside the framework of government, but with the blessing of the Foundation, has been free to choose its members, settle its priorities, formulate its programme, and present and follow up its reports as it judges best.

A personal note in conclusion

The success of the Nuffield Council has been mainly due to the outstanding calibre of those who readily agreed to serve on it or on one of its working parties, and to the high quality of the secretariat staff. I pay tribute to them. A more significant tribute, however, was the decision in 1994 by the Medical Research Council and the Wellcome Trust to share the costs of the Council with the Nuffield Foundation. So long as funding can continue, the Nuffield Council on Bioethics should continue – fulfilling a role in which there is little or no prospect of the Government replacing it. Its future tasks cannot be predicted; but the pace of advanced biomedical and biological research is unlikely to slacken and the study of ethical issues should keep pace. The early years of the Council have shown that it is a challenge which can best be met by an independent body with the expertise, experience and authority for the task – and also that without such a body it might not be met at all.

Health
care as
a public
service

Albert Weale
Professor of Government, University of Essex

The main facts about the comparative political economy of
health care are massively simple. Measured as a proportion of
national income, spending on medical care rises as national income
rises. Health care spending in the aggregate thus behaves more like
a luxury good than a necessity. Institutional arrangements modify in
predictable ways the position of individual countries around the

regression line that links health and wealth. So, systems with single payers spend less than systems with multiple payers for any given level of income. Closing off direct access to specialists also makes a difference to levels of spending. But all systems face rising pressures on health care spending stemming from a complex mixture of demography, technology and higher expectations.

To say that the facts are simple is not to say that their discovery and validation have been easy, still less to say that they are unimportant. Indeed, absorbing their implications is something that few societies have even begun to contemplate, let alone deal with adequately. Robert Maxwell has performed the service of not only detailing the empirical relationships between health and wealth but also of leading the process of thinking about the implications of the trends that modern research has uncovered.[1] By a mixture of quiet advocacy, Socratic questioning, careful analysis and the sort of institutional and financial diplomacy that the chief executives of major foundations need to do their jobs, he has done as much as anyone to persuade people to think about the ethical implications of the modern political economy of health.

One question underlies all the other ethical issues. Can the principle on which modern health care systems is based still be justified in the light of evidence about spending patterns? That principle can be easily stated. It is that comprehensive, high-quality medical care should be available to all citizens on test of professionally judged medical need and without financial barriers to access. Does our understanding of the political economy of modern medicine and the relationship between health and wealth call into question this principle?

Let us call the conception of health care corresponding to this principle the conception of health care as a public service. A public service may be defined as any institution in society that both shapes the fundamental conditions under which members of society interact with one another and offers its services to citizens as citizens, applying only further qualifications or tests that all citizens might be expected to meet. For example, the functioning of a legal system operating on principles of due process is a public service in this sense. So is an educational system that provides equality of opportunity for children. And so is a high-quality health care system constructed in accordance with the requirements of comprehensiveness and availability.

How might we justify such a conception of health care? It is this question that I shall be concerned with in this essay. In principle, there are two sorts of argument to which we can appeal: want-regarding arguments, which consider the wants that people have and ask how they can be met by various types of institution, and ideal-regarding arguments, which consider how certain ideals of social life are to be embodied in the basic institutions of a society. Between them, these two forms of argument span a wide range, as Brian Barry showed some years ago.[2]

There is one traditional argument for health care as a public service, which appeals to the idea that there is market failure in respect of medical services. This is a standard want-regarding type of argument. An argument of this sort goes some way towards the model of health as a public service, but, I shall argue, not nearly far enough. To complete the justification we need an ideal-regarding argument and, in particular, we need to appeal to one specific ideal, namely that the basic institutions of a society should be so constructed as to enable citizens to conduct their interactions with one another on terms in which personal dignity is respected and enhanced. It is this concern for personal dignity that lies behind the distributional concerns that form the principled basis for modern health care systems. Public services are thus social institutions that embody certain social and political ideals. A health system on the model of a public service is one way of embodying the social ideal of equal dignity and respect in public life.

I shall conduct the argument in two stages. First, I seek to undermine the adequacy of the 'market failure' argument for publicly provided health care. Second, I consider the ideal of personal dignity and its implications.

The market failure rationale

The most common argument for state involvement in health care is derived from the idea of market failure. The general concept of market failure originated in Pigou's *The economics of welfare*,[3] but it has since been extensively elaborated and now is available in textbook form to account for the institutions of the welfare state.[4]

In many forms of policy argument, the concept of market failure is often used loosely to refer to all those features of market societies that sensitive souls profess to abhor. However, in Pigou's original analysis the concept of market failure had a quite precise sense, and for the sake of clarity, if nothing else, we should stick to this sounder usage. Strictly speaking, a market failure occurs when a particular market fails to achieve an allocation of resources in which no one can be made better off without making anyone else worse off. The situation in which no one can be made better off without making anyone else worse off is known, after the inventor of the concept Vilfredo Pareto, as a Pareto optimum. Thus, we can say that a market failure is one in which markets fail to achieve a Pareto optimum.

In standard neo-classical economic theory it is possible to show that if markets satisfy certain conditions, then their competitive equilibrium (roughly defined as a situation in which no trader in the market has an incentive to change his or her behaviour given the behaviour of all other traders) will always produce a Pareto optimal allocation of resources. The most visible signs of a Pareto optimum are that there are no queues for scarce resources at the same time as there are unsold goods on the shelves. Conversely, the combination of a shortage of goods in demand and a lack of demand for goods in plentiful supply is a sign of economic inefficiency. Under the former Communist regimes of central and eastern Europe, the existence of unsaleable goods alongside queues for unavailable goods was the clearest evidence that too many resources were going into some lines of economic activity and too little into others. The fundamental claim of neo-classical economic theory is that, provided that certain conditions are satisfied, market forms of production will not create such inefficient outcomes. In this sense, markets are efficient.

The problem is that the conditions under which markets achieve this result are so stringent that not only are they not met in the real world, but it is also impossible to think that they could be met in the real world.[5] They include the following: no increasing returns to scale in production; perfect information, or at least no significant asymmetries of information among traders; no spill-overs from one set of trades to another, for example in the form of polluting activity; and free entry and exit by potential providers into various lines of activity. In many markets, of course, the departures from these assumptions in practice are not so serious as to cause practical worries about the extent of economic inefficiency that they generate. However, in health care the situation is different.

The two key conditions that cause the problems are related. They are the existence of asymmetries of information between health care suppliers and health care consumers, and the barriers to entry into medical professions created in order to control the quality of care. Together, these conditions mean that clinicians necessarily have considerable autonomy of behaviour and that consumers are often likely to make the wrong purchases. Indeed, the existence of professional autonomy means that even knowledgeable consumers like insurance companies that take on the burden of purchasing health care for individuals are likely to make the wrong purchases, since they are not in a position to monitor some of the crucial practices of health care professionals. In particular, the suitability of specific diagnostic tests or clinical interventions is difficult to monitor, and may lead to overpurchase or inflated billing.[6]

Given this asymmetry of information, the medical care market is unlikely to achieve an efficient allocation of resources. This is compounded by the existence of spill-over effects, particularly in relation to infectious diseases. Vaccinations, housing improvements and the quality of water supplies are all likely to be undersupplied in a market, given that the benefits of the improvements are generally available as pure public goods, but the costs of provision fall on individuals. In these circumstances few individuals will have an incentive to make a contribution to the provision of the public good sufficient to generate an optimal supply.

The twin expectation is, therefore, that a private market in health care will typically oversupply expensive high-tech medicine and undersupply public health care, including sanitation, housing improvements and vaccinations. In other words, market failure in health care means that we arrive at a situation not unlike the suppression of markets in most commodities in Communist societies, where some goods were oversupplied and others undersupplied.

I have tried to state the market failure argument in relation to health care as simply and pungently as I can. I do not have any dissension from the argument as far as it goes. My claim is simply that it does not go far enough and, in particular, that it does not yield the principle that informs modern health care systems, namely that comprehensive, high-quality care should be available to all citizens on test of professionally judged medical need.

If we rely solely on the market failure argument, we cannot derive the idea of a public service but merely that of a regulated market. Some think it possible to finesse this later stage of the argument by invoking the economic theory of transactions costs. On this theory we explain forms of economic organisation (not the allocation of resources) as a response to three features of social life: bounded rationality, opportunistic behaviour and asset specificity.[7] Bounded rationality means that people's information is limited. Opportunistic behaviour means that people will take advantage when they can. And asset specificity means that people have their marketable skills tied up in one line of activity and may not easily be able to transfer them to another. The implications of these three features of economic life together or in some combination, it is claimed, provide a rationale for health as a public service.

To see how this sort of argument might work, consider the phenomenon of the overuse of diagnostic tests in health care markets.

This can arise as a result of the asymmetry of information between insurer and clinician (a consequence of bounded rationality) and the existence of opportunistic behaviour (the willingness to take advantage to one's own benefit when suitable conditions present themselves). One way of dealing with this problem, the transactions cost theorist would argue, is to establish health as a public service in which diagnostic procedures are subject to direct administrative control, possibly supplemented by attempts to internalise an ethos of responsibility among practitioners held accountable within the public service for their behaviour. To be sure, this is a possible line of argument. Yet, it clearly trades very heavily on certain contingent features of comparisons between markets and publicly administered systems that may not bear much scrutiny. In particular, the assumption that it is sensible to establish a whole form of organisation in order to deal with such a particular problem seems implausible.

However, the failure to establish a public service rationale is only one part of the difficulty in the argument. The other serious difficulty is that market failure has in itself nothing to do with the distribution of resources. All the market failure argument says is that, given an initial allocation of resources, a market in health will not achieve a Pareto optimum after all mutually advantageous trades have taken place. It says nothing about whether the initial allocation of resources can be justified in the first place. The simplest way to see this is to note that there may be many possible Pareto efficient allocations of resources in an economy corresponding to all the possible initial allocations of resources. Thus, although distributive failure is often mentioned as an element of market failure, it is strictly irrelevant to the evaluation of such failure, since all that the theory of market failure is about is how well markets enable people to move from an initial allocation of resources to an efficient allocation, not with whether that initial allocation is in any way fair or justified.

One way in which some people have tried to bridge this gap in the argument is to say that, since people care about one another, some redistribution of resources will itself be Pareto efficient, because it will make both the recipient and the donor better off. Donors, however, will need to be reassured that other potential donors are not free-riding on the efforts of some, and so public funding is called for.[8] There are many possible problems with this argument, but in the present context all we need to note is that its most natural institutional embodiment would be a system of free care available for the poor on test of means, not a system of health care on the model of a public service.

This general insensitivity to issues of distribution in arguments drawn from modern welfare economics is not surprising. Welfare economics is the heir to 19th century utilitarianism, and utilitarianism, taken strictly, is merely the injunction to maximise welfare independently of any distributive considerations. Both Bentham[9] and Sidgwick,[10] in similar ways, had to supplement the utilitarian principle with a principle of equality, but as Richard Braithwaite once remarked of Sidgwick, this amounts to sweetening the pure milk of the utilitarian gospel.[11]

In general, then, the most plausible form of want-regarding argument cannot yield any distributive principles unless one is also prepared to make additional assumptions about the right of all persons to have their wants put on the same plane, and this additional assumption has to be introduced as an independent axiom. But this is to introduce a certain ideal of society and of the place of citizens in a society, and so, once we take into account this extra, independent axiom, we find ourselves involved in arguments of a quite different type.

An ideal-regarding argument

Markets are embodied in larger forms of social organisation. Since we cannot rely on the market failure argument alone to get us to the idea of health care as a public service, we have to draw upon a larger conception of society, and the social ideals with which it may be associated. One particular ideal is that the basic institutions of a society should embody the conditions of dignity for all its members. This means that no one should have their self-respect undermined by the normal functioning of social institutions. Equal dignity precludes privilege for some and second-class status for others. A health care system on the model of public service is one way of embodying that ideal in public life.

Why should this be so? How does it come about that one way of embodying the ideal of equal dignity is that health care should be modelled on the principles of a public service? Part of the answer to this question is to say that health is a need, and in this sense basic to a person's welfare. A form of social organisation that failed to address such needs would undermine the conditions of self-respect on which a sense of dignity depends. This argument needs to be spelt out in more detail, however.

The principle underlying modern health care systems had three elements: availability, quality and comprehensiveness. The link between the principle of equal dignity and these three elements is direct in some cases, but less direct in others. There are obvious direct links in the requirement that high-quality health care be available to all. After all, if equal dignity is at issue, then to make health care available to some, but not to all, would be a direct assault on that principle. Note that in this formulation there is no implication that medical care facilities, such as hospitals and health centres, have to be publicly owned, let alone a requirement that health care professionals should be public employees. It is quite compatible with this principle to separate purchaser and provider, so long as any system in which the split is entrenched meets the condition of universal availability.

Indeed, the distinction between the principle of availability and the particular forms of organisation that health care might take is important if we are to take the ideal of dignity seriously. Although the public ownership of health care facilities may be one way in which universal availability is secured, there is now enough work on the spatial and other barriers to access on publicly owned systems to enable us to say that public ownership of itself is insufficient to meet the requirements of accessibility. Although health care as a public service embodies an ideal, it is possible for institutional performance to fall short of that ideal and so to be judged deficient by reference to it.

Just as there is a direct connection between the principle of equal dignity and the concept of availability, so there is a direct connection between the ideal of dignity and the concept of high-quality care. For example, were public institutions to embody a distinction between the quality of care that one citizen receives compared with the quality that another receives, then there is not only a difference of service between the two cases, but also the insult to the person who receives less favourable treatment, since their needs are thought to be less worthy than the needs of someone else. Moreover, when differences of treatment run systematically along class or ethnic lines, then the insult is the greater since it resonates with the wider inequalities of citizenship that still disfigure societies.

In contrast with the concepts of availability and quality, the connection between the idea of dignity and the principle of comprehensiveness is more indirect and difficult to establish. The problem arises because a stress on comprehensiveness seems at odds with the need for rationing that is inseparable from modern health care systems.

For all the reasons that Robert Maxwell has stressed in his various writings on the subject, the need for rationing in modern health care systems is inescapable.[12] Improvements in medical technology, rising expectations of care and demographic shifts in population mean that it is now no longer credible to claim that all patients at all times can have access to all forms of medical intervention that can potentially do some good. Yet, if we insist that the principle of comprehensiveness is central to the idea of health as a public service, we seem to encounter a contradiction. How can we meaningfully speak about a comprehensive health care system and acknowledge the need to ration?

Part of the answer is of course to try to blunt the edge of the conflict by insisting that what can responsibly be promised under the heading of comprehensive health care is care that is effective. Comprehensive health care on this understanding cannot mean the provision of placebos or snake-medicine, particularly expensive placebos or snake-medicine. Yet, even when we have eliminated all the procedures and therapies that do not meet the test of effectiveness, we are still likely to find that we have to ration.

In these circumstances one argument is that the only way in which we can deal with the problem of rationing is to institute a core or basic range of services that are publicly guaranteed, so that people can be sure at least of their entitlements within that range. Yet such a move would seem to be at odds with the principle of comprehensiveness. If only a core range of services is available, can we meaningfully speak about comprehensiveness of care? Can a health care system really be said to offer comprehensive care if it excludes, say, treatment for infertility, certain types of joint replacements, gender reassignment or drug regimes with a low, but nevertheless definite, probability of success?

At this point we could simply say that there is a conflict between comprehensiveness and feasibility which has to be resolved as best it can be in practice by the judgement of those responsible for making public policy. Moreover, rationing implies some limitation on the range of treatments that can be offered, but some argue that it is unwise to make the trade-off too explicit for fear of damaging the perception that the National Health Service is comprehensive in scope. In many ways this approach has been the traditional response of the British health policy-makers to the dilemmas implicit in seeking to run a comprehensive health service at the same time as recognising the problem of rationing. There is a great deal to be said in favour of this traditional approach. However, I wonder whether the problem can be dealt with only in this surreptitious way. Perhaps there is an alternative tack that it may be worth taking.

Given the need to ration, we clearly cannot hold to the strongest possible notion of comprehensiveness, namely that all that technically could be provided for everyone should be provided for everyone, since that is an impossible requirement. We shall need to weaken the requirement by saying that comprehensiveness means that all that it is reasonable to provide should be part of practice of the health care system. The term 'reasonable' here is obviously open to various interpretations, and no doubt there will be disagreement as to what it means exactly. However, whatever it means, the test of reasonableness is itself subject to certain constraints, one of which is that in its application it should respect the requirement of equal dignity. To see what this implies, consider what logical procedures we might use to define reasonableness in the relevant sense.

One such procedure would be to impose certain conditions on what would count as a reason for modifying the comprehensiveness principle in its literal technical sense. Thus, a restriction of comprehensiveness would not be reasonable, in the sense that it met the equal dignity condition, if it excluded services in some way that made particular classes of individual, identified in non-clinical ways, especially disadvantaged. For example, it is not in accordance with the equal dignity principle to exclude treatments for conditions, such as Tay-Sach disease or sickle cell anaemia, that are specific to certain ethnic groups. On the other hand, it would be acceptable on the equal dignity test to exclude certain sorts of treatments because the ratio of their cost to their benefit was extremely high.

The difference between the two cases is clear. Where treatment for a condition specific to an ethnic group is excluded, a society is saying to some of its members that it is not concerned about their lives. When highly expensive therapies are excluded, however, a society is not saying to its members that it is unconcerned, but rather that the concern cannot be acted on at a cost that leaves other social ideals sufficiently intact. If I know that there are some conditions to which anyone is liable that will not form part of what is agreed to be in the list of reasonably comprehensive care, then I simply know that not all that technically can be done sensibly should be done. I cannot object to that: neither I nor anyone else is wronged by that decision. On the other hand, if I know that a society is ignoring a problem because it is only a problem for a minority, then I know that a wrong is being done, whether I am in the minority or not.

This way of looking at things runs into one obvious difficulty. What is wrong with defining the notion of reasonably comprehensive in such a way that its content is terribly Spartan? After all, if the only test

216

that has to be met is that the rules under which exclusions are made should be ones that potentially apply to all in a society, someone might claim that the health care anyone needs is modest in both scope and range. Reasonably comprehensive is thus definable in a potentially very narrow way. Dignity in hardship is still dignity after all.

In this context, the crucial question is whether the Spartan conditions are in fact likely to be shared by all, in which case they may be justified, or whether they are not simply an excuse to substitute the principle of a basic publicly assured minimum, above which people are free to fend for themselves, for the principle of comprehensive care. If the intention is to make such a substitution, then this would be disallowed by the principle of equal dignity, which implies that all should enjoy comparable conditions of dignity for social institutions taken as a whole. If one were looking for a behavioural test that distinguished between these two cases, then an obvious one to apply is to see whether a large number of people who could afford financially to exit from the public system nevertheless choose not to do so because they find the comprehensiveness of the coverage adequate.

I have argued that the dignity principle is sufficient to justify a public service conception of health care, but is it also necessary? Do we have to invoke such a principle to derive the conclusion that the public service model is justifiable? Someone might say that all we needed was the notion of equal want-satisfaction attached to the traditional market failure argument. However, this is surely insufficient. Equal want-satisfaction is a purely arithmetical notion with no moral content or force unless it is attached to an idea of what the moral basis is for saying that everyone is entitled to treatment on the same terms. That conclusion would seem to require something at least as strong as the principle of equal dignity.

Conclusion

The principle that all members of society should enjoy personal dignity in their treatment by the basic institutions of society is a distributive principle. Moreover, it is a principle of substance, contrasting with and excluding certain other principles, such as the principle that people are entitled to satisfy whatever wants they happen to have and can afford to pay for, or the principle that the members of a society are entitled only to a basic minimum of care above which they have to fend for themselves.

Yet, while having the right form and force, the principle is not self-evident. Although the widespread public support for the basic principles of the National Health Service which shows up in every public opinion poll that is ever conducted on the subject suggests that the concept is widely shared, it is certainly not universally held. Its cultural origin is undoubtedly religious. It is particularly associated, in one of its most influential forms, with the Quaker principle that the light of God was to be found in everyone. That belief, it seems to me, has been secularised into the principle of the dignity of persons and the importance of treating persons not merely as means but also as ends in themselves. Whether the moral force of this belief can survive its secularisation is, of course, another – and much deeper – question that I have not attempted to deal with here.

References and notes

1. Maxwell RJ. *Health and wealth*. Lexington (Mass.): DC Heath and Co., 1981.
2. Barry B. *Political argument*. London: Routledge and Kegan Paul, 1965.
3. Pigou AC. *The economics of welfare*. London: Macmillan, 1920.
4. Barr N. *The economics of the welfare state*. 2nd edn. London: Weidenfeld and Nicholson, 1993.
5. Rowley R, Peacock A. *Welfare economics: a liberal restatement*. Oxford: Martin Robertson, 1975.
6. Reinhardt UE. Resource allocation in health care: the allocation of lifestyles to providers. *The Milbank Quarterly* 1987; 65(2):153–76.
7. Williamson OE. *Economic organisation*. Brighton: Harvester-Wheatsheaf, 1986.
8. Compare Culyer AJ. *The political economy of social policy*. Oxford: Martin Robertson, 1980 (especially pp. 64–9).
9. Jeremy Bentham's principle, as reported by John Stuart Mill, was that of 'everybody to count for one, and nobody for more than one'. See: Mill J S. Utilitarianism. In: Mill J S. *On liberty and other essays*. Oxford: Oxford University Press, 1991, p. 199.

10. Sidgwick H. *The methods of ethics*. 6th edn. London: Macmillan, 1901.
11. Braithwaite RB. *The theory of games as a tool for the moral philosopher*. Cambridge: Cambridge University Press, 1955.
12. Maxwell RJ. Why rationing is on the agenda. *British Medical Bulletin* 1995; 51(4):761–8.